Silent Complicity: State Sovereignty, Global Inaction, and the Rwandan Genocide

Kayumba David

Published by Kayumba David, 2024.

While every precaution has been taken in the preparation of this book, the publisher assumes no responsibility for errors or omissions, or for damages resulting from the use of the information contained herein.

SILENT COMPLICITY: STATE SOVEREIGNTY, GLOBAL INACTION, AND THE RWANDAN GENOCIDE

First edition. November 2, 2024.

Copyright © 2024 Kayumba David.

ISBN: 979-8227583871

Written by Kayumba David.

Also by Kayumba David

Grow a Backbone and Walk out of an Abusive Marriage
HARVESTING ILLUSIONS: The Global Greed and the Pan-African Paradox
Hope and Healing: A Chaplain's Handbook
HOW TO FAIL A CONTINENT: THE WESTERN GUIDE TO SUPPORTING DICTATORS AND LOOTING RESOURCES IN AFRICA
REVERSING TYPE 2 DIABETES NATURALLY
Visas: The Irony of Freedom
A MEETING WITH MAJESTY: THE KING'S CALL TO HUMANITY
A MEETING WITH MAJESTY: THE KING'S CALL TO HUMANITY
Visas: The Irony of Freedom
Grow a Backbone and Walk Out: The Guide to Escaping Your Abusive Marriage
Love Beyond Time A Comedy of Divine Connection
Silent Complicity: State Sovereignty, Global Inaction, and the Rwandan Genocide

Watch for more at www.zcews.org.

Table of Contents

Silent Complicity: State Sovereignty, Global Inaction, and the Rwandan Genocide 1
   Dedication 3
   Preface 4
   Part I: Historical Roots and the Path to Genocide 6
   Part II: The Genocide and Global Complicity 7
   Part III: Aftermath and Rebuilding Rwanda 9
   Part IV: Lessons and Reflections 10
   Part I: Historical Roots and the Path to Genocide 11
   Introduction 12
   Part II: The Genocide and Global Complicity 29
   Part III: Aftermath and Rebuilding Rwanda 58
   Part IV: Lessons and Reflections 83

Dedication

To the resilient people of Rwanda, who rose from the ashes with strength and determination, and to the people of Uganda, whose unwavering support of the Rwandan Patriotic Front (RPF) helped bring hope and a future to a nation in despair.

Silent Complicity: State Sovereignty, Global Inaction, and the Rwandan Genocide

Kayumba David

Copyright © 2024 by Kayumba David

Dedication

To the resilient people of Rwanda, who rose from the ashes with strength and determination, and to the people of Uganda, whose unwavering support of the Rwandan Patriotic Front (RPF) helped bring hope and a future to a nation in despair.

Preface

The Rwandan genocide of 1994 remains an indelible scar on the conscience of the global community. As a human rights advocate and scholar deeply invested in the intersections of state power and human dignity, I felt compelled to revisit this pivotal moment in history, not just as an academic inquiry but as a call to action for humanity. This book is an evolution of my Master's dissertation, *State Sovereignty Versus Individual Rights in the Case of the Rwanda Genocide, 1994*, presented at Nkumba University in 2006 under the guidance of Dr. Michael Mawa. In it, I initially explored the complex dynamic between the sanctity of state sovereignty and the moral imperative to protect human life.

Over the years, as I continued my work in social justice, theology, and diplomacy, the lessons from Rwanda became a driving force behind my advocacy for human rights and my belief in the necessity of international intervention when governments fail to protect their citizens. This book is not just a historical account; it is a declaration that the right to life should supersede the principle of state sovereignty when these values clash.

I have included a chapter honoring the RPF for its extraordinary efforts in rebuilding Rwanda after the genocide. It is a testament to the power of leadership rooted in reconciliation, justice, and progress. The incredible transformation of Rwanda, from near-total collapse to a beacon of hope and economic progress, showcases not only the resilience of the Rwandan people but also what is possible when a nation is guided by visionary governance.

I hope that this work will serve as both a reminder and a rallying cry: that "Never Again" is not just a phrase but a responsibility that must be upheld by all nations, especially when the sanctity of human life is at risk.

Kayumba David

Brussels, 2024

Content

Introduction: From Dissertation to Declaration

- Origins of the Book

Part I: Historical Roots and the Path to Genocide

The Roots of Division – Rwanda's Political and Social History

- Rwanda's Pre-Colonial Society
- Colonial Manipulation and the Creation of Ethnic Identities
- The Hutu Revolution and Independence
- Rise of Juvénal Habyarimana and Consolidation of Hutu Power
- The Formation of the Rwandan Patriotic Front (RPF)
- The 1990 RPF Invasion and the Escalation of Tensions
- The Arusha Accords and Political Crisis

The Spark Ignites – The Assassination of President Habyarimana

- Background to the Assassination
- Habyarimana's Death as a Convenient Pretext
- Pre-Genocide Preparations and Propaganda
- The Immediate Aftermath of the Assassination
- International Reactions and Inaction

Part II: The Genocide and Global Complicity

A Genocide Unleashed – The Massacre Begins

- Organized Violence and Systematic Killings
- The Role of Local Leaders and Militia Groups
- Massacres in Churches, Schools, and Villages
- The Role of Ordinary Citizens in the Genocide

The Machinery of Death – Media, Propaganda, and Hate Speech

- The Role of Radio Télévision Libre des Mille Collines (RTLM)
- Anti-Tutsi Propaganda and Dehumanization
- Propaganda's Role in Mobilizing Killers
- International Awareness of the Propaganda Campaign

International Complicity: The Price of Indifference

- The United Nations' Failure to Act
- The United States and Reluctance to Intervene
- France's Involvement and Operation Turquoise
- The Role of Belgium and the International Community
- The Consequences of Global Non-Action

Power Politics and the Ethics of Non-Intervention

- Sovereignty vs. Responsibility to Protect
- The Influence of National Interests in Foreign Policy
- International Debates on Intervention

- The Cost of Inaction and Ethical Dilemmas

Part III: Aftermath and Rebuilding Rwanda

After the Genocide: A Broken Nation

- The Human and Social Toll of Genocide
- Psychological Impact on Survivors and Perpetrators
- Infrastructure and Economic Collapse
- The Refugee Crisis and Repatriation

Justice for Genocide: The ICTR and Gacaca Courts

- The Establishment of the International Criminal Tribunal for Rwanda (ICTR)
- Successes and Criticisms of the ICTR
- Rwanda's Gacaca Courts: Community Justice and Reconciliation
- Challenges in Achieving Justice and Healing

From Ashes to Ascendancy – Rwanda's Remarkable Rebirth

- The RPF's Strategy for Reconciliation
- Post-Genocide Governance and Political Stability
- Economic Growth and Infrastructure Development
- Social and Cultural Rebuilding
- Rwanda's Transformation as a Model for Recovery

Part IV: Lessons and Reflections

Lessons for the Future: State Sovereignty Versus Human Rights

- Reflection on Sovereignty and Human Rights
- The Responsibility to Protect Doctrine
- The Role of International Law in Preventing Genocide
- Applying the Lessons of Rwanda to Future Conflicts

A Call to Action: Preventing Future Genocides

- Revisiting "Never Again" as a Global Imperative
- Strengthening Global Human Rights Mechanisms
- Improving International Response Systems
- The Role of Civil Society, Education, and Advocacy

Conclusion: The Price of Silence and the Call for Change

- Summarizing the Consequences of Global Inaction
- Renewing the Commitment to Human Rights
- A Vision for a World Where "Never Again" Holds True

Bibliography

Part I: Historical Roots and the Path to Genocide

Introduction

From Dissertation to Declaration

This book is a continuation and expansion of my Master's dissertation, *State Sovereignty Versus Individual Rights in the Case of the Rwanda Genocide, 1994,* which I presented at Nkumba University in 2006 under the esteemed supervision of Dr. Michael Mawa. My dissertation initially explored the delicate tension between the traditional principle of state sovereignty and the undeniable need to protect individual rights in situations where lives are threatened by state-led or state-sanctioned violence. Over the years, as I delved deeper into human rights advocacy, this tension became a call to action, pushing me to expand my academic work into a broader critique of the global response—or lack thereof—to the genocide in Rwanda.

In 1994, Rwanda became the stage for one of the most horrific episodes of mass violence in modern history, as nearly one million people were murdered in a systematic and ruthless genocide. The Rwandan genocide was marked not only by the brutality and efficiency of the killings but also by the chilling silence of the international community. Despite early warnings and mounting evidence of an unfolding catastrophe, the world's most powerful nations and international institutions failed to intervene. The result was a deadly combination of complicity through inaction, bureaucratic paralysis, and political prioritization of national interests over human life.

The core argument of this book is simple yet profound: in circumstances where human life is at risk, the international community must be willing to transcend traditional concepts of state sovereignty. The events of 1994 revealed that state sovereignty, while fundamental in international law, cannot serve as an impenetrable barrier protecting regimes and actors who perpetrate or permit crimes against humanity. The responsibility to protect human life should take precedence over respecting a state's territorial integrity when that state is either unable or unwilling to protect its own people.

This book endeavors to achieve two main goals. Firstly, it holds the international community accountable for its role in the Rwandan genocide, examining how political, economic, and strategic concerns outweighed the moral imperative to save lives. It is crucial to analyze the actions—and inactions—of key players, including the United Nations, the United States, France, and Belgium, all of whom failed to act decisively. Each chapter unpacks the layers of diplomatic failures, bureaucratic indecision, and ethical compromises that allowed the genocide to reach such devastating proportions.

Secondly, this book is not merely an examination of the past but a call for a fundamental shift in how we understand and apply the principles of humanitarian intervention. The Rwandan genocide exemplifies the urgent need for international reform and the adoption of a global framework that prioritizes the protection of human rights over strict adherence to non-interference. The principle of "Responsibility to Protect" (R2P), developed in the years following the genocide, was inspired in part by the failure in Rwanda. However, this principle has yet to be fully realized or universally enforced, and recent global events show that the world has not fully embraced the lessons of 1994.

This book includes a chapter dedicated to Rwanda's remarkable recovery under the leadership of the Rwandan Patriotic Front (RPF). The RPF's decision to focus on reconciliation and reconstruction rather than retribution allowed Rwanda to rise from the ashes of genocide and develop into one of Africa's most resilient and rapidly growing nations. The story of Rwanda's transformation provides an example of how effective leadership, patience, and a commitment to national unity can heal even the deepest wounds. Rwanda's rebirth is a testament to the resilience of its people and the possibilities that exist when a nation is united in purpose and vision.

Ultimately, *Silent Complicity: State Sovereignty, Global Inaction, and the Rwandan Genocide* is not merely a historical account. It is a plea to the international community to remember Rwanda and to commit to preventing future genocides by prioritizing the sanctity of human life over the principle of non-interference. I invite readers to reflect on this tragedy and to consider the moral responsibility that comes with global power. The legacy of Rwanda demands that we do better, that we act with urgency and compassion, and that we do not allow the lessons of 1994 to be forgotten.

Through the lens of Rwanda, this book offers a call for a world where human rights take precedence, where every life is valued, and where "Never Again" is not just a slogan but a commitment that defines global action.

1

The Roots of Division – Rwanda's Political and Social History

The Rwandan genocide of 1994 was not an isolated event; it was deeply rooted in a long history of political manipulation, colonial intervention, and entrenched social divisions. This chapter explores the historical context that set the stage for the genocide, tracing Rwanda's social and political history from pre-colonial times to the period of independence, and examining the persistent marginalization of the Tutsi population. Through historical analysis and scholarly perspectives, this chapter provides a comprehensive look at how colonialism, post-colonial politics, and ethnic divisions contributed to a foundation of tension and violence.

Rwanda's Pre-Colonial Society: Fluid Identities and Centralized Power

In pre-colonial Rwanda, the terms "Hutu" and "Tutsi" did not signify rigid ethnic categories but rather indicated social and economic distinctions. According to Jan Vansina, pre-colonial Rwandan society was characterized by a highly centralized political structure, governed by the Mwami (king), who ruled over a society in which wealth and occupation largely determined one's social status rather than fixed ethnic identities (Vansina, 2001, p. 45). Tutsis were often pastoralists, typically associated with cattle herding, while Hutus were predominantly agriculturalists.

This social stratification was flexible, with some degree of social mobility; Hutus could acquire wealth and become associated with the Tutsi class, and similarly, impoverished Tutsis could be classified as Hutu (Prunier, 1995, p. 26). As Mahmood Mamdani argues, "In pre-colonial Rwanda, the distinction between Hutu and Tutsi was not strictly an ethnic one; it was a matter of economic and social function" (Mamdani, 2001, p. 50). This fluidity in social structure, however, would later be manipulated by colonial powers to create a more rigid ethnic divide.

Colonial Manipulation and the Creation of Ethnic Identities

The arrival of European colonizers, first the Germans in the late 19th century and later the Belgians after World War I, transformed Rwandan society profoundly. The Belgians, influenced by racial pseudoscience, viewed the Tutsi minority as racially superior due to their taller stature and physical appearance, which they deemed closer to "European" (Des Forges, 1999, p. 40). This perception led the Belgians to favor the Tutsis, placing them in administrative roles and granting them privileged access to education and economic opportunities.

Belgian authorities institutionalized ethnic identity by introducing identity cards in the 1930s, which classified individuals as Hutu, Tutsi, or Twa based on ancestry and physical characteristics (Prunier, 1995, p. 44). This classification system "transformed what had once been flexible social distinctions into rigid, almost caste-like identities" (Mamdani, 2001, p. 90). Alison Des Forges points out that this policy "crystallized divisions that had previously been fluid, setting the stage for future conflict by politicizing ethnicity" (Des Forges, 1999, p. 53).

The colonial administration's favoritism created resentment among the Hutu majority, who began to see the Tutsi not merely as wealthier pastoralists but as a privileged ruling class aligned with colonial power. This division would be further exacerbated by colonial policies that placed the Tutsi in positions of authority over the Hutu population, effectively embedding a sense of ethnic hierarchy and oppression.

The Hutu Revolution and Independence: Rising Tensions and Marginalization

The late 1950s saw the rise of anti-colonial and nationalist movements across Africa, including Rwanda. Amid this wave of change, the Belgian colonial administration began to shift its support toward the Hutu majority, fearing that the privileged Tutsi elite would align with independence movements (Des Forges, 1999, p. 76). In 1959, an anti-Tutsi uprising, known as the "Hutu Revolution," erupted. Hutu leaders advocated for a democratic government, which they argued would reflect the Hutu majority's interests and end Tutsi dominance.

The revolution marked a turning point in Rwandan history. Between 1959 and 1962, thousands of Tutsis were killed, and hundreds of thousands were forced into exile in neighboring countries, primarily Uganda, Burundi, and the Democratic Republic of Congo (Prunier, 1995, p. 88). Rwanda gained independence in 1962, and the newly established Hutu-led government, led by President Grégoire Kayibanda, institutionalized policies that further marginalized Tutsis, limiting their access to education, political participation, and employment.

Mahmood Mamdani explains that "The revolution of 1959 was not just a rebellion against colonial rule; it was also a rejection of the Tutsi dominance that had become associated with colonial privilege" (Mamdani, 2001, p. 135). The new government institutionalized ethnic quotas, cementing a system of discrimination that would persist for decades. The Tutsi minority, now viewed as an ethnic "other" and labeled as enemies of the state, faced systematic repression that left them politically and economically marginalized.

The Rise of Juvénal Habyarimana and the Consolidation of Hutu Power

In 1973, General Juvénal Habyarimana, a Hutu from northern Rwanda, led a coup that ousted Kayibanda. Habyarimana's government, though initially promising stability and national unity, soon entrenched ethnic divisions and intensified anti-Tutsi policies. Habyarimana established the National Republican Movement for Democracy and Development (MRND), a single-party state that institutionalized Hutu dominance. According to Scott Straus, "Habyarimana's regime consolidated power by perpetuating ethnic divisions and aligning the state with the Hutu identity" (Straus, 2006, p. 67).

The Habyarimana government was marked by an atmosphere of increasing hostility toward Tutsis, who were systematically excluded from political and economic life. Anti-Tutsi propaganda became state policy, with government media portraying Tutsis as inherently untrustworthy and as a threat to the Hutu majority's power. Filip Reyntjens notes that "Habyarimana's rule exploited the fears of the Hutu majority, solidifying ethnic hatred that would later fuel genocidal violence" (Reyntjens, 2013, p. 46).

During this period, the Tutsi diaspora in Uganda and other neighboring countries continued to grow. Many exiled Tutsis lived as stateless refugees, facing discrimination in their host countries. The Rwandan government's refusal to address the refugee crisis and allow the exiled Tutsis to return created an enduring grievance among the diaspora, particularly among young exiled Tutsis who felt alienated and stateless.

The Formation of the Rwandan Patriotic Front (RPF)

The increasing marginalization of Tutsis in Rwanda, coupled with the grievances of the diaspora, led to the formation of the Rwandan Patriotic Front (RPF) in 1987. Led by Fred Rwigyema and Paul Kagame, the RPF was composed primarily of young Tutsi exiles who had grown up in Uganda and participated in the Ugandan Bush War alongside Yoweri Museveni. The RPF aimed to overthrow Habyarimana's government, end the discriminatory policies against Tutsis, and secure the right of return for the Tutsi diaspora.

As Linda Melvern explains, "The RPF represented the frustrated aspirations of Tutsi exiles who sought not only the right to return to Rwanda but also an end to the oppressive regime that had marginalized them for decades" (Melvern, 2000, p. 87). The RPF's military and political goals were perceived by the Habyarimana government as an existential threat, and the regime intensified anti-Tutsi rhetoric, branding all Tutsis within Rwanda as potential collaborators of the RPF.

The 1990 RPF Invasion and the Escalation of Tensions

On October 1, 1990, the RPF launched an invasion from Uganda into Rwanda, marking the beginning of a civil war that would last until the genocide in 1994. The Habyarimana government responded to the RPF invasion with a state of emergency, cracking down on Tutsi civilians and imprisoning thousands under suspicion of collaborating with the rebels. The government also intensified anti-Tutsi propaganda, branding all Tutsis as traitors and the "enemy within" (Des Forges, 1999, p. 112).

The government-controlled media, particularly the *Kangura* newspaper, published inflammatory articles urging Hutus to be vigilant against Tutsi "infiltrators" and "cockroaches." According to Scott

Straus, this propaganda "mobilized the population and created an environment where violence against Tutsis was viewed as both necessary and patriotic" (Straus, 2006, p. 95).

The Arusha Accords and Growing Tensions

In 1993, after years of conflict, the Rwandan government and the RPF signed the Arusha Accords, a peace agreement intended to end the civil war and create a power-sharing government. The Accords were widely resented by Hutu extremists, who saw the agreement as a concession to Tutsi rebels. Extremists within Habyarimana's regime actively opposed the peace process, viewing the Accords as a threat to Hutu hegemony.

Mamdani asserts that "The Arusha Accords were viewed by Hutu extremists as a betrayal, heightening tensions and fueling the extremist belief that the only solution was the elimination of the Tutsi threat" (Mamdani, 2001, p. 198). This opposition to peace laid the groundwork for what would become the final and most devastating act of violence in Rwandan history.

Conclusion

By the early 1990s, Rwanda was a deeply divided nation with a volatile political climate. The colonial manipulation of ethnic identities, the rise of Hutu power, and the sustained marginalization of the Tutsi population created a powder keg of tension. The 1990 RPF invasion intensified these divisions, and the signing of the Arusha Accords only served to deepen the animosity of Hutu extremists who saw peace as a threat to their dominance. These historical and social factors, combined with years of propaganda and repression, set the stage for the genocide that would soon follow.

References

- Des Forges, Alison. *Leave None to Tell the Story: Genocide in Rwanda.* Human Rights Watch, 1999.
- Kinzer, Stephen. *A Thousand Hills: Rwanda's Rebirth and the Man Who Dreamed It.* John Wiley & Sons, 2008.
- Mamdani, Mahmood. *When Victims Become Killers: Colonialism, Nativism, and the Genocide in Rwanda.* Princeton University Press, 2001.
- Melvern, Linda. *A People Betrayed: The Role of the West in Rwanda's Genocide.* Zed Books, 2000.
- Prunier, Gérard. *The Rwanda Crisis: History of a Genocide.* Columbia University Press, 1995.
- Straus, Scott. *The Order of Genocide: Race, Power, and War in Rwanda.* Cornell University Press, 2006.
- Vansina, Jan. *Le Rwanda Ancien: Le Royaume Nyiginya.* Karthala, 2001.

2

The Spark Ignites – The Assassination of President Habyarimana

The assassination of Rwandan President Juvénal Habyarimana on April 6, 1994, is often cited as the immediate trigger for the Rwandan genocide. However, the genocide was not a spontaneous reaction to Habyarimana's death; rather, it was the culmination of months, if not years, of meticulous planning by Hutu extremists. This chapter examines the assassination of Habyarimana and highlights how this event provided the final pretext for unleashing a genocide that had already been carefully prepared, with weapons stockpiled, propaganda disseminated, and militias trained and ready to act.

Background to the Assassination: A Tense and Divided Nation

By early 1994, Rwanda was already in a state of political and social unrest. The Arusha Accords, signed in 1993 to bring an end to the civil war between the government and the Rwandan Patriotic Front (RPF), called for power-sharing arrangements and the integration of Tutsi exiles and RPF fighters into Rwandan society. However, many Hutu extremists saw these accords as a threat to Hutu supremacy and a betrayal of their political interests. As Linda Melvern notes, "The Arusha Accords threatened the established power structure, and the hardliners in the regime were determined to thwart any concessions to the Tutsi minority" (Melvern, 2000, p. 108).

Opposition to the peace process was fierce within the Hutu extremist faction, particularly among members of Habyarimana's inner circle, known as the *Akazu*. They feared that the implementation of the Arusha Accords would diminish their control and allow Tutsis and Hutu moderates into positions of power. According to Mahmood Mamdani, the *Akazu* and other hardline factions "saw any compromise as a sign of weakness, and they increasingly viewed the Tutsi population, both inside and outside Rwanda, as a threat to Hutu dominance" (Mamdani, 2001, p. 179).

The political climate was volatile, and anti-Tutsi propaganda was disseminated widely through government-controlled media, including the infamous *Radio Télévision Libre des Mille Collines* (RTLM). This propaganda painted Tutsis as a dangerous enemy, dehumanizing them as "cockroaches" and inciting the Hutu population to prepare for violence. Alison Des Forges writes, "By early 1994, RTLM broadcasts and other propaganda outlets had conditioned ordinary Hutus to see Tutsis as the 'enemy within,' preparing the population psychologically for the genocide" (Des Forges, 1999, p. 62).

The Assassination of Habyarimana: A Convenient Pretext for Genocide

On the evening of April 6, 1994, Habyarimana's plane was shot down as it approached Kigali International Airport, killing him and everyone on board, including the President of Burundi, Cyprien Ntaryamira. The assassination remains a point of contention, with some sources suggesting that the RPF was responsible, while others point to Hutu extremists within Habyarimana's own government. Regardless of who was responsible, the assassination became the immediate justification for unleashing a campaign of mass killing against Tutsis and moderate Hutus.

In her comprehensive account of the genocide, Melvern argues, "Habyarimana's death provided the extremists with the perfect pretext they needed to launch a genocide that had already been meticulously planned" (Melvern, 2000, p. 112). Within hours of the plane crash, Hutu extremists mobilized and began executing their plan with chilling efficiency. They established roadblocks throughout Kigali and began systematically identifying and killing Tutsis and moderate Hutus.

Roméo Dallaire, the head of the United Nations Assistance Mission for Rwanda (UNAMIR), later recounted his frustration and horror as events unfolded. "The extremists were prepared. They had everything in place. The killing started immediately, as though the entire country had been waiting for a signal" (Dallaire, 2003, p. 121). Dallaire had previously warned the UN of potential genocidal intentions within the government but received no substantive support or reinforcements. The assassination of Habyarimana triggered the activation of pre-existing plans, and the killing machinery moved into action.

Pre-Genocide Preparations: A Well-Orchestrated Plan for Mass Murder

The speed and efficiency of the killings that followed Habyarimana's death indicate that the genocide was not a spontaneous outbreak of ethnic hatred but rather a carefully organized and orchestrated campaign. Hutu extremists had been preparing for the genocide for months, if not years. Stockpiles of weapons, including machetes, grenades, and firearms, had been amassed and distributed throughout the country. Alison Des Forges documents how "huge quantities of machetes had been imported into Rwanda, and the killers were already well-prepared to implement the plans that had been laid out" (Des Forges, 1999, p. 93).

The *Interahamwe* militia, a paramilitary group affiliated with the ruling MRND party, played a central role in the genocide. Members of the *Interahamwe* had been trained in military tactics and indoctrinated with anti-Tutsi ideology, preparing them to kill with brutal efficiency. As Prunier writes, "The *Interahamwe* were not a disorganized mob;

they were well-trained, disciplined, and prepared to carry out their orders" (Prunier, 1995, p. 156).

Furthermore, lists of Tutsis and Hutu moderates were compiled in advance, indicating that the genocide was premeditated. Scott Straus notes that "these lists allowed the killers to identify and target specific individuals quickly, suggesting a level of planning that is rarely seen in cases of mass violence" (Straus, 2006, p. 103). The existence of these lists, coupled with the rapid establishment of roadblocks across the capital, underscores the organized nature of the killing campaign.

The Role of Propaganda: Weaponizing Words to Mobilize Killers

The genocide was facilitated not only by weapons and trained killers but also by a powerful propaganda campaign that prepared ordinary citizens to participate in the massacres. *Radio Télévision Libre des Mille Collines* (RTLM) broadcasted hate-filled messages that urged Hutus to take up arms against the Tutsis, calling them "cockroaches" that needed to be exterminated. Melvern describes the role of RTLM as "instrumental in spreading hatred and inciting violence. It was as much a weapon as any machete" (Melvern, 2000, p. 135).

The propaganda reached beyond Kigali, permeating rural areas and convincing ordinary Hutu civilians that killing Tutsis was a patriotic act. According to Philip Gourevitch, "The media's message was clear: to protect Rwanda from the Tutsi threat, Hutus had a duty to kill" (Gourevitch, 1998, p. 92). This indoctrination was essential to mobilizing large segments of the population to participate in the genocide, transforming neighbors into killers.

The impact of propaganda on the populace cannot be understated. Mamdani notes, "The propaganda transformed social relations, making mass murder not only conceivable but justifiable" (Mamdani, 2001, p. 220). By the time Habyarimana's plane was shot down, the groundwork for genocide had been laid; the people were psychologically prepared to take part in the atrocities that would unfold over the next three months.

Immediate Aftermath: The Onset of Mass Killing

Within hours of Habyarimana's assassination, Kigali descended into chaos. Roadblocks were set up across the city, and Tutsis attempting to flee were intercepted and killed. In neighborhoods, homes were raided, and entire families were massacred. The speed and scale of the violence were unprecedented; as Des Forges observes, "The killing spread with terrifying speed, sweeping across the country as if a carefully orchestrated wave" (Des Forges, 1999, p. 132).

Ordinary civilians, many of whom had been incited to hatred through months of propaganda, were encouraged to take part in the massacres. Local government officials and community leaders organized groups of civilians, arming them with machetes and other weapons. Straus highlights that "the role of local leaders was crucial in mobilizing the population, and many civilians participated in the killings under orders from these leaders" (Straus, 2006, p. 127).

The organized nature of the killings underscores that this was not a spontaneous uprising but a deliberate, state-sanctioned extermination campaign. The role of the *Interahamwe* and other militias, as well as the rapid establishment of a "killing infrastructure," demonstrates that the genocide was planned down to the smallest detail.

International Response: Silence and Inaction

Despite the clear signs that a genocide was underway, the international response was alarmingly slow. The United Nations and the international community had been warned of the risk of mass atrocities months before the assassination. Roméo Dallaire, head of UNAMIR, had even sent a cable to UN headquarters in January 1994, warning of potential genocide plans and requesting additional support. His warnings, however, went unheeded. Dallaire later lamented, "We had the information, and we had the capacity to act, but the world chose to look away" (Dallaire, 2003, p. 143).

The reluctance of the United States and other major powers to label the crisis as "genocide" further hindered any meaningful intervention. Alan Kuperman argues that "bureaucratic inertia and political concerns prevented the international community from acting decisively, even as the death toll mounted" (Kuperman, 2001, p. 58). The Security Council ultimately reduced UNAMIR's mandate and withdrew a significant number of peacekeepers at the height of the crisis, leaving Rwanda virtually abandoned.

Conclusion: The Assassination as a Trigger, Not a Cause

The assassination of President Habyarimana provided the immediate pretext for the genocide, but it was not the cause. The killing infrastructure, propaganda campaigns, and armed militias were already in place, and the genocide had been meticulously planned well in advance. As Mamdani reflects, "The assassination was merely a trigger that unleashed the violence for which the groundwork had been laid over years of propaganda and hate" (Mamdani, 2001, p. 225).

The events following Habyarimana's death reveal the horrifying consequences of inaction and complicity. The failure of the international community to intervene in time allowed the genocide to unfold unchecked, resulting in the deaths of nearly one million people. The assassination was the spark, but the fire of genocide had been prepared long before.

References

- Des Forges, Alison. *Leave None to Tell the Story: Genocide in Rwanda.*

Human Rights Watch, 1999.
- Dallaire, Roméo. *Shake Hands with the Devil: The Failure of Humanity in Rwanda*. Random House Canada, 2003.
- Gourevitch, Philip. *We Wish to Inform You That Tomorrow We Will Be Killed with Our Families: Stories from Rwanda*. Picador, 1998.
- Kuperman, Alan. *The Limits of Humanitarian Intervention: Genocide in Rwanda*. Brookings Institution Press, 2001.
- Mamdani, Mahmood. *When Victims Become Killers: Colonialism, Nativism, and the Genocide in Rwanda*. Princeton University Press, 2001.
- Melvern, Linda. *A People Betrayed: The Role of the West in Rwanda's Genocide*. Zed Books, 2000.
- Prunier, Gérard. *The Rwanda Crisis: History of a Genocide*. Columbia University Press, 1995.
- Straus, Scott. *The Order of Genocide: Race, Power, and War in Rwanda*. Cornell University Press, 2006.

Part II: The Genocide and Global Complicity

3

A Genocide Unleashed – The Massacre Begins

The assassination of President Habyarimana on April 6, 1994, was the signal for a genocide that had been meticulously planned. Within hours of the president's death, Rwandan society was engulfed in violence, and a campaign of systematic extermination against the Tutsi population, as well as moderate Hutus, was set in motion. This chapter examines the early stages of the genocide, including the rapid mobilization of the Hutu militias, the establishment of roadblocks, and the organized killing of civilians. It also discusses the role of local leaders, community mobilization, and the horrifying participation of ordinary civilians in the slaughter.

Organized Violence and Systematic Killings

From the outset, it was clear that the genocide was not an uncoordinated outbreak of violence but rather a carefully planned operation. Roadblocks were erected throughout Kigali and other major towns, manned by militia members who systematically checked the identity cards of passersby, singling out Tutsis and moderates for execution. The speed with which these checkpoints were established indicated the pre-planned nature of the genocide. As Alison Des Forges writes, "The setting up of roadblocks and the immediate killings of Tutsis across Kigali revealed the level of preparation; this was not spontaneous rage but a calculated extermination" (Des Forges, 1999, p. 147).

Local officials and military leaders played a significant role in organizing the massacres. In some cases, they provided lists of Tutsi families and prominent individuals, ensuring that the killings were systematic and widespread. Gérard Prunier notes that "The administrative system, down to the local level, was harnessed to carry out genocide with brutal efficiency. Civil servants and local officials used their authority to mobilize the population and coordinate the killing" (Prunier, 1995, p. 178).

One of the most shocking aspects of the Rwandan genocide was the involvement of ordinary civilians. Many Hutus were pressured or coerced into participating, while others willingly joined the killing out of fear, hatred, or peer pressure. Philip Gourevitch reflects on this phenomenon, writing, "The Rwandan genocide was a true people's war; it was fought with machetes, clubs, and rocks by neighbors against neighbors, by family members against each other" (Gourevitch, 1998, p. 138).

The Role of the *Interahamwe* and Hutu Militias

The *Interahamwe*, a paramilitary group affiliated with the ruling MRND party, played a central role in carrying out the genocide. Trained and indoctrinated with anti-Tutsi ideology, members of the *Interahamwe* were ruthless and efficient in their operations. Scott Straus notes that "The *Interahamwe* were the foot soldiers of the genocide, carrying out the massacres with an organization and discipline that showed the extent of premeditation" (Straus, 2006, p. 112). The militia was often supported by soldiers from the Rwandan Armed Forces (FAR), who supplied weapons, vehicles, and sometimes participated directly in the killings.

Members of the *Interahamwe* and other militias, such as the *Impuzamugambi*, were frequently deployed to remote villages where they would gather local residents and incite them to kill their Tutsi neighbors. According to Des Forges, "The militia members, often working with local officials, led the massacres in rural areas, ensuring that no Tutsi communities were spared" (Des Forges, 1999, p. 159). They used machetes, clubs, grenades, and firearms to carry out their atrocities, and they often tortured their victims before killing them, instilling terror and exerting control over the local population.

Massacres in Churches, Schools, and Hospitals

Throughout Rwanda, churches, schools, and hospitals, which were traditionally places of refuge, became sites of mass slaughter. In many cases, Tutsis gathered in these locations, hoping for sanctuary, only to be betrayed by the priests, teachers, or administrators who either directly participated in or facilitated the massacres. Prunier describes the betrayal of sanctuary as one of the darkest aspects of the genocide: "The killers showed no respect for the traditional sanctuaries, and the very places where people sought safety became slaughterhouses" (Prunier, 1995, p. 190).

In some instances, clergy members actively collaborated with the killers. Scott Straus documents cases where priests and nuns handed over Tutsi refugees to the militia or even led the massacres themselves. He writes, "The participation of church leaders in the killings profoundly shocked survivors, stripping away any remaining hope that sanctuary could be found" (Straus, 2006, p. 124).

One of the most notorious massacres occurred at the Nyarubuye Roman Catholic Church, where thousands of Tutsis who had gathered for safety were brutally killed over the course of several days. Des Forges recounts a survivor's testimony: "We thought that maybe the church would save us. But when they began to kill, there was no mercy. The ground was soaked in blood" (Des Forges, 1999, p. 168).

The Role of Ordinary Citizens in the Genocide

The Rwandan genocide is particularly unsettling because it involved large-scale participation by ordinary civilians. In many communities, Hutu villagers joined the killings, often attacking their Tutsi neighbors and even family members. Propaganda had dehumanized Tutsis as "cockroaches" and portrayed them as a threat to Hutu survival, leading many to believe that killing was justified. Mahmood Mamdani reflects on this chilling aspect, stating, "What made the Rwandan genocide particularly horrific was the fact that ordinary people, manipulated by state propaganda and fear, became perpetrators" (Mamdani, 2001, p. 214).

In some cases, civilians participated out of coercion or fear of retribution from militias, but in many other instances, they were willing participants. As Philip Gourevitch describes, "It was not just a matter of survival; many were swept up in a frenzy of hatred, greed, and the promise of seizing property" (Gourevitch, 1998, p. 145). The social and psychological pressures to participate were intense, as refusal to join the killings could result in accusations of sympathy with the Tutsis and subsequent punishment.

The involvement of ordinary citizens not only increased the scale of the genocide but also tore apart Rwanda's social fabric. Communities were left devastated, as neighbors turned against neighbors and families were destroyed. The genocide would leave behind a legacy of trauma and distrust that would endure for generations.

Coordination from Local Authorities

The Rwandan government's involvement in the genocide extended far beyond national leaders and military forces; it permeated down to local authorities and officials, who played a critical role in coordinating the massacres. The administrative hierarchy in Rwanda was deeply involved in organizing and executing the genocide, with governors, mayors, and village leaders instructing their communities to participate in the killings. Alison Des Forges explains, "Local government officials were pivotal in mobilizing and directing the population, making the genocide a nationwide campaign involving the entire state apparatus" (Des Forges, 1999, p. 172).

These local officials wielded enormous influence over the population, and in many cases, they were able to persuade or compel civilians to participate in the killing campaigns. Prunier notes that "The genocide could not have been as thorough or widespread without the active involvement of local administrators, who used their authority to carry out orders and facilitate mass violence" (Prunier, 1995, p. 198). This coordination from the local level was crucial in extending the genocide to every corner of the country.

Psychological Impact of the Genocide on Survivors

The Rwandan genocide left profound psychological scars on survivors, many of whom witnessed the murder of family members, friends, and neighbors. The traumatic experiences left survivors with long-lasting psychological effects, including depression, post-traumatic stress disorder (PTSD), and complex grief. Philip Gourevitch describes the haunting memories survivors carry: "For the survivors, the memories are inescapable. They live with the weight of loss and the horrors they have seen" (Gourevitch, 1998, p. 213).

The brutality of the genocide and the intimate nature of the violence created unique challenges for the survivors, many of whom struggled to reintegrate into communities where they had witnessed or experienced horrific acts. Scott Straus notes, "The trauma inflicted by the genocide went beyond physical wounds; it left deep psychological scars on individuals and communities" (Straus, 2006, p. 141). The psychological aftermath of the genocide continues to affect survivors, impacting Rwanda's efforts at reconciliation and rebuilding.

International Community's Response During the Initial Stages of the Genocide

As the genocide unfolded, the international community remained largely passive. Reports of massacres and widespread violence reached the United Nations and Western governments, but the response was muted. Alan Kuperman explains that "bureaucratic inertia and political concerns in Western capitals led to a paralysis, as leaders failed to act in the face of clear evidence of genocide" (Kuperman, 2001, p. 74).

The reluctance of major powers to label the crisis as genocide further hindered any substantive intervention. Roméo Dallaire, head of the United Nations Assistance Mission for Rwanda (UNAMIR), was frustrated by the lack of support from the international community. "We were there, we saw the horrors, and yet the world remained indifferent. It was one of the darkest failures of our time" (Dallaire, 2003, p. 203). The international community's failure to act during the early stages of the genocide allowed the killings to continue unimpeded, ultimately leading to the deaths of nearly one million people.

Conclusion: A Nation Engulfed in Bloodshed

The initial stages of the Rwandan genocide revealed the extent of premeditation and the role of local organization in carrying out the massacres. With the backing of the government, local leaders, and militias, ordinary Rwandans were mobilized to participate in a campaign of extermination that would leave the country devastated. Churches, schools, and hospitals turned into sites of horror, and the very social fabric of Rwanda was torn apart as neighbors and families turned on each other.

The international community's inaction allowed the genocide to escalate, despite clear evidence of systematic killing. As the world looked on, nearly one million lives were lost, and Rwanda was left scarred and broken. This chapter underscores the brutal reality of the genocide's early days and the devastating impact of silence and complicity.

References

- Des Forges, Alison. *Leave None to Tell the Story: Genocide in Rwanda*. Human Rights Watch, 1999.
- Dallaire, Roméo. *Shake Hands with the Devil: The Failure of Humanity in Rwanda*. Random House Canada, 2003.
- Gourevitch, Philip. *We Wish to Inform You That Tomorrow We Will Be Killed with Our Families: Stories from Rwanda*. Picador, 1998.
- Kuperman, Alan. *The Limits of Humanitarian Intervention: Genocide in Rwanda*. Brookings Institution Press, 2001.
- Mamdani, Mahmood. *When Victims Become Killers: Colonialism, Nativism, and the Genocide in Rwanda*. Princeton University Press, 2001.
- Prunier, Gérard. *The Rwanda Crisis: History of a Genocide*. Columbia University Press, 1995.
- Straus, Scott. *The Order of Genocide: Race, Power, and War in Rwanda*. Cornell University Press, 2006.

4

The Machinery of Death – Media, Propaganda, and Hate Speech

One of the most insidious aspects of the Rwandan genocide was the role played by media and propaganda in mobilizing the population to commit acts of unspeakable violence. The Hutu-led government, with the complicity of extremist media outlets, systematically dehumanized the Tutsi population, spreading hate speech and incitement to genocide. This chapter examines how propaganda, especially through the radio and print media, laid the psychological groundwork for mass violence. It also explores the role of specific media figures, the messages they propagated, and the mechanisms of hate speech that turned ordinary citizens into killers.

The Rise of Propaganda: Demonizing the Tutsi Population

The use of propaganda to incite violence against the Tutsi population began well before the start of the genocide. Hutu extremists, particularly those aligned with the *Akazu*—the inner circle around President Habyarimana—used media as a tool to stir up fear and hatred. The *Kangura* newspaper, which was established in 1990, became a prominent voice in the campaign against Tutsis, publishing inflammatory articles that labeled Tutsis as "cockroaches" and painted them as an existential threat to Hutu power.

One of the most infamous examples of propaganda appeared in the December 1990 issue of *Kangura*, which published the "Ten Commandments of the Hutu," a manifesto that called on Hutus to shun Tutsis, denounce intermarriages, and treat Tutsis as enemies of the state. As Linda Melvern explains, "The Ten Commandments sought to reinforce the image of Tutsis as foreign invaders, fundamentally alien and dangerous" (Melvern, 2000, p. 75). By framing the Tutsi as an existential threat, the *Kangura* newspaper fueled a perception among Hutus that violence against Tutsis was both justified and necessary.

According to Mahmood Mamdani, this dehumanization was a deliberate strategy that laid the groundwork for genocide. He notes, "The Tutsis were portrayed as a fifth column, an internal enemy aligned with the RPF, whose very existence endangered Hutu survival" (Mamdani, 2001, p. 187). This systematic othering transformed Tutsis from fellow citizens into "the other," creating a narrative that justified extermination.

The Role of Radio Télévision Libre des Mille Collines (RTLM)

The most notorious medium for spreading hate and incitement was Radio Télévision Libre des Mille Collines (RTLM), established in 1993. RTLM became a powerful voice in Rwanda, reaching audiences across the country and using colloquial language, jokes, and popular music to connect with listeners. RTLM's broadcasts were far from neutral; they carried explicit messages encouraging Hutus to kill their Tutsi neighbors and presented Tutsis as "inyenzi," or cockroaches, who needed to be eradicated.

According to Alison Des Forges, "RTLM played a central role in the genocide, broadcasting not only hate-filled messages but also providing operational information, such as the locations of people who needed to be 'dealt with'" (Des Forges, 1999, p. 60). RTLM hosts, such as Georges Ruggiu, a Belgian national, and Hassan Ngeze, openly called for violence against Tutsis, often identifying individuals by name and instructing listeners on where they could find their Tutsi neighbors.

Philip Gourevitch emphasizes the impact of RTLM, stating, "It was not just a source of information, it was a call to arms. RTLM turned ordinary citizens into soldiers of hate" (Gourevitch, 1998, p. 142). By combining hate speech with tactical guidance, RTLM blurred the line between media and militia, functioning as both an ideological weapon and a practical tool of genocide.

Weaponizing Words: The Language of Dehumanization

The language used by Hutu extremists in their propaganda was carefully crafted to strip Tutsis of their humanity. Terms such as "inyenzi" (cockroaches) and "ibyitso" (accomplices) were used consistently to portray Tutsis as subhuman and to justify violence against them. This language, pervasive in RTLM broadcasts and *Kangura* publications, was not just inflammatory; it was designed to normalize killing and create a social environment in which murder became a patriotic act.

Scott Straus notes, "The use of dehumanizing language made it psychologically easier for Hutus to participate in the killings, as they were encouraged to see Tutsis not as people but as pests that needed extermination" (Straus, 2006, p. 118). Dehumanization is a common precursor to genocide, as it breaks down social and moral barriers that would otherwise prevent individuals from participating in mass violence.

As Linda Melvern argues, "The constant repetition of words like 'cockroach' and 'enemy' had a desensitizing effect, conditioning the population to accept extreme violence as a necessary measure" (Melvern, 2000, p. 97). This desensitization allowed for the systematic slaughter of Tutsis and provided a moral justification for those who participated in the genocide.

Mobilizing Ordinary Citizens: The Influence of Media on the Population

The power of propaganda in Rwanda went beyond simply spreading hate; it mobilized ordinary citizens to actively participate in the genocide. Through constant broadcasts and incendiary newspaper articles, the media created an environment in which killing was seen as a civic duty. Mamdani reflects on the chilling effectiveness of propaganda, noting that "the Rwandan genocide was unique in its reliance on grassroots participation, enabled by a media machine that convinced people they were acting in the nation's interest" (Mamdani, 2001, p. 201).

RTLM was particularly effective in reaching rural populations, where access to other sources of information was limited. Local leaders and militia members used RTLM broadcasts to organize and direct the killings. As Alison Des Forges observes, "In many rural areas, RTLM was the only source of information, and its influence was absolute. When RTLM called for action, people responded" (Des Forges, 1999, p. 125).

The role of local leaders and government officials in reinforcing media messages further strengthened the impact of propaganda. Local officials would sometimes accompany militia members, echoing the language of RTLM to ensure compliance. Des Forges provides an account of one official telling his community, "If you do not kill the Tutsis, you too will be killed as a traitor" (Des Forges, 1999, p. 130). This combination of propaganda and coercion created an environment of fear and hatred, where participation in the genocide became both a social expectation and a survival tactic.

International Awareness and Inaction

The international community was aware of the role that Rwandan media, particularly RTLM, played in inciting violence. Reports from journalists, diplomats, and NGOs highlighted the dangerous rhetoric being broadcasted. The United Nations peacekeeping mission in Rwanda, led by General Roméo Dallaire, sent urgent warnings to UN headquarters about RTLM's incitement to genocide, but these warnings were largely ignored. Dallaire recounts his frustration, writing, "We knew that RTLM was inciting genocide, yet the world failed to act. It was as though the international community was deaf to our pleas" (Dallaire, 2003, p. 192).

Despite clear evidence of hate speech and incitement, there was little international intervention to shut down RTLM or halt the publication of *Kangura*. Alan Kuperman criticizes this inaction, arguing, "The failure to intervene and halt the propaganda machine allowed the genocide to proceed unchecked, with devastating consequences" (Kuperman, 2001, p. 63). The international community's failure to address the propaganda problem allowed the machinery of hate to continue, fueling the genocide and contributing to the loss of nearly one million lives.

The Aftermath: Accountability for Media Incitement

Following the genocide, efforts were made to hold those responsible for inciting violence accountable. Key figures in the Rwandan media, including Hassan Ngeze, founder of *Kangura*, and Ferdinand Nahimana, a founding member of RTLM, were prosecuted by the International Criminal Tribunal for Rwanda (ICTR). They were charged with genocide, incitement to genocide, and crimes against humanity. The ICTR's convictions marked a significant moment in international law, establishing that media figures could be held criminally responsible for inciting genocide.

The ICTR found that "the broadcasts of RTLM and the publications of *Kangura* constituted direct and public incitement to commit genocide" (ICTR, Case No. ICTR-99-52-T, 2003). This landmark ruling underscored the power of media in shaping perceptions and mobilizing people to commit atrocities. Alison Des Forges notes, "The ICTR's convictions of Ngeze, Nahimana, and others sent a message to the world that incitement to genocide is a crime, and that those who use media as a weapon of hate will be held accountable" (Des Forges, 1999, p. 303).

Conclusion: The Power and Danger of Propaganda

The Rwandan genocide revealed the terrifying potential of media to incite mass violence. Through radio broadcasts and newspaper articles, propaganda laid the psychological groundwork for genocide, creating a culture in which violence against Tutsis was not only accepted but encouraged. The role of RTLM and *Kangura* illustrates how dehumanizing language, repeated frequently enough, can turn ordinary citizens into killers.

The failure of the international community to intervene and halt the incitement highlights the global responsibility to recognize and act against hate speech. The ICTR's prosecution of media figures after the genocide underscores the importance of accountability, setting a precedent that incitement to genocide is a prosecutable offense under international law. As Linda Melvern writes, "The Rwandan genocide was a lesson in the deadly power of propaganda, one that the world must remember if we are to prevent future atrocities" (Melvern, 2000, p. 152).

References

- Des Forges, Alison. *Leave None to Tell the Story: Genocide in Rwanda*. Human Rights Watch, 1999.
- Dallaire, Roméo. *Shake Hands with the Devil: The Failure of Humanity in Rwanda*. Random House Canada, 2003.
- Gourevitch, Philip. *We Wish to Inform You That Tomorrow We Will Be Killed with Our Families: Stories from Rwanda*. Picador, 1998.
- ICTR, Case No. ICTR-99-52-T. *The Prosecutor v. Ferdinand Nahimana, Jean-Bosco Barayagwiza, and Hassan Ngeze*. Judgment, December 3, 2003.

- Kuperman, Alan. *The Limits of Humanitarian Intervention: Genocide in Rwanda*. Brookings Institution Press, 2001.
- Mamdani, Mahmood. *When Victims Become Killers: Colonialism, Nativism, and the Genocide in Rwanda*. Princeton University Press, 2001.
- Melvern, Linda. *A People Betrayed: The Role of the West in Rwanda's Genocide*. Zed Books, 2000.
- Straus, Scott. *The Order of Genocide: Race, Power, and War in Rwanda*. Cornell University Press, 2006.

5

International Complicity – The Price of Indifference

The Rwandan genocide stands as one of the most horrific failures of the international community to prevent mass atrocity. Despite clear warnings and overwhelming evidence of genocidal intent, the international response was marked by indifference, bureaucratic inertia, and political calculations that prioritized national interests over humanitarian concerns. This chapter explores the inaction of the United Nations, the United States, France, Belgium, and other international actors who had the power to intervene but chose not to. It examines the reasons behind their inaction and the devastating consequences of their failure to respond decisively to Rwanda's cries for help.

The United Nations' Failure to Act

The United Nations' response to the genocide was a textbook example of bureaucratic paralysis. Despite having a peacekeeping mission on the ground, the United Nations Assistance Mission for Rwanda

(UNAMIR), the UN failed to prevent or halt the violence. UNAMIR, under the command of Canadian General Roméo Dallaire, had a limited mandate that prevented it from taking any action beyond monitoring the ceasefire between the Rwandan government and the Rwandan Patriotic Front (RPF). When the genocide began, the mission's restricted rules of engagement meant that it was virtually powerless to intervene.

In January 1994, months before the genocide, General Dallaire sent a "genocide fax" to the UN headquarters in New York, warning of Hutu extremists' plans for mass killings and asking for additional troops and resources. The response from the UN was tepid, and his requests for reinforcements were denied. In his memoir, *Shake Hands with the Devil*, Dallaire recalls his frustration and horror at the UN's inaction, writing, "We had the information, we had the capacity to act, yet the world looked away as Rwanda descended into chaos" (Dallaire, 2003, p. 92).

The Security Council's failure to act decisively was largely influenced by the reluctance of key member states, particularly the United States, to commit to another peacekeeping mission in Africa. The recent failure of a peacekeeping operation in Somalia had left the United States and other nations wary of becoming entangled in another African conflict. Alison Des Forges emphasizes this point, stating, "The shadow of Somalia hung over every decision regarding Rwanda. The international community was not prepared to take any risks" (Des Forges, 1999, p. 101).

The UN's response to the unfolding genocide reached a nadir when the Security Council voted to reduce UNAMIR's forces from 2,500 to a mere 270 troops at the height of the killings. Gérard Prunier highlights this moment as a critical failure, writing, "By withdrawing most of its troops, the UN essentially abandoned Rwanda to its fate, allowing the massacres to continue unimpeded" (Prunier, 1995, p. 137).

The United States: Reluctance to Intervene

The United States' reluctance to intervene in Rwanda stemmed from a combination of political, strategic, and bureaucratic concerns. The debacle in Somalia in 1993, where eighteen American soldiers were killed in a failed operation, heavily influenced U.S. foreign policy toward Africa. Fear of another high-profile failure made the U.S. government cautious about committing troops to a complex African conflict.

Internal memos from the U.S. State Department revealed a deliberate decision to avoid using the term "genocide" in reference to Rwanda, as this label would have legally obligated the United States to take action under the Genocide Convention. Samantha Power, in her book *A Problem from Hell: America and the Age of Genocide*, writes, "The United States deliberately avoided acknowledging genocide in Rwanda to evade the responsibility to act. The fear of entanglement trumped any moral imperative" (Power, 2002, p. 382).

The U.S. government's inaction was further compounded by bureaucratic inertia. Power quotes an internal memo from the State Department stating, "Our policy is not to interfere in Rwanda, as we have no national interest at stake" (Power, 2002, p. 389). This cold calculation exemplifies how national interest was prioritized over humanitarian duty, resulting in the failure to act against one of the worst genocides of the 20th century.

France's Role: Complicity and the Question of National Interests

France's involvement in Rwanda before and during the genocide has been widely criticized. As Rwanda's primary ally and arms supplier, France had a vested interest in maintaining Hutu control, particularly because of its close relationship with Habyarimana's government. France provided financial and military support to the Rwandan government, seeing it as a strategic ally in the Francophone sphere of influence in Africa.

During the genocide, France launched *Opération Turquoise*, a military intervention ostensibly aimed at establishing a "safe zone" in southwestern Rwanda. However, the operation has been heavily criticized for its true motives and its failure to prevent further massacres. Many accused France of using the operation to protect its allies within the Hutu government and to facilitate the escape of genocidal leaders. According to Linda Melvern, "Opération Turquoise was a thinly veiled attempt to shield France's allies, not an impartial mission to save lives" (Melvern, 2000, p. 203).

French historian Gérard Prunier writes, "The French intervention did little to stop the killings. Instead, it created a corridor through which genocidal forces could flee into Zaire, effectively allowing them to escape justice" (Prunier, 1995, p. 215). The establishment of the safe zone in French-controlled areas allowed Hutu extremists to regroup and escape prosecution, leading to years of instability in the region.

Belgium: A Colonial Legacy and an Early Withdrawal

Belgium, the former colonial power in Rwanda, was also deeply implicated in the events leading up to the genocide. As the primary contributor to UNAMIR's peacekeeping forces, Belgium had a significant presence in Rwanda. However, when ten Belgian peacekeepers were brutally murdered in the early days of the genocide, Belgium immediately withdrew its troops, severely weakening UNAMIR's capacity to protect civilians.

The Belgian withdrawal was a critical blow to UNAMIR, as it reduced the mission's manpower and left Rwandans vulnerable. Samantha Power describes Belgium's decision as "a tragic abdication of responsibility. The withdrawal sent a message to the genocidal forces that the international community would not intervene" (Power, 2002, p. 374). Belgian policymakers feared that public outcry over the deaths of their soldiers would erode domestic support for the mission, leading them to prioritize national political concerns over humanitarian needs.

Belgium's colonial history in Rwanda also cast a shadow over its decision-making. Belgium had historically exacerbated ethnic divisions in Rwanda by favoring the Tutsi minority, and this legacy left Belgian leaders ambivalent about intervening in the conflict. Alison Des Forges writes, "Belgium's colonial history and the recent tragedy of its soldiers influenced its decision to disengage from Rwanda, further isolating a nation in crisis" (Des Forges, 1999, p. 82).

The Consequences of Global Inaction

The failure of the international community to intervene in Rwanda had catastrophic consequences. By the time the genocide ended in July 1994, nearly one million Tutsis and moderate Hutus had been slaughtered. The lack of action allowed the violence to continue unchallenged, emboldening the perpetrators and creating an environment where the killing could proceed unchecked.

As Roméo Dallaire reflected, "The world abandoned Rwanda, and that abandonment cost countless lives. It was a failure of humanity on every level" (Dallaire, 2003, p. 315). The international community's unwillingness to prevent or stop the genocide became a source of profound shame and guilt, leading to widespread criticism and calls for reform in international humanitarian policy.

The genocide in Rwanda prompted an international reckoning over the doctrine of humanitarian intervention. Many questioned the efficacy of the UN's peacekeeping system and called for stronger mechanisms to prevent future atrocities. Samantha Power argues, "Rwanda exposed the limitations of existing frameworks for intervention and highlighted the need for a new approach to protect human rights" (Power, 2002, p. 412).

Reflections on Responsibility: "Never Again" Reconsidered

In the aftermath of the Holocaust, the world had vowed "Never Again." The Rwandan genocide, however, revealed that this commitment was more rhetorical than practical. The failure of the international community to act decisively in Rwanda forced a painful reassessment of the concept of responsibility in cases of mass atrocity. As Linda Melvern writes, "The world's response to Rwanda was a betrayal of the principles it claimed to uphold. The promise of 'Never Again' was hollow in the face of bureaucratic indifference and self-interest" (Melvern, 2000, p. 256).

The Rwandan genocide has since influenced the development of the Responsibility to Protect (R2P) doctrine, which asserts that the international community has a moral duty to intervene when a state fails to protect its citizens from genocide, war crimes, ethnic cleansing, or crimes against humanity. Mahmood Mamdani reflects on this shift, arguing that "Rwanda forced the world to confront the limitations of state sovereignty when human rights are at stake. R2P is a response to the failure in Rwanda, an attempt to prevent future atrocities" (Mamdani, 2001, p. 318).

The lessons of Rwanda continue to resonate in global discussions about intervention and humanitarian responsibility. The genocide serves as a reminder of the high cost of inaction and the need for vigilance, compassion, and decisive action when human lives are at stake.

Conclusion: The Price of Indifference

The international community's failure to act in Rwanda remains one of the most shameful episodes in modern history. The UN's bureaucratic paralysis, the United States' political reluctance, France's conflicted intervention, and Belgium's immediate withdrawal all contributed to the unimpeded progress of the genocide. As nearly one million people were slaughtered, the world looked on, unwilling or unable to intervene.

The consequences of this indifference have shaped the discourse on human rights and intervention. The genocide in Rwanda serves as a powerful reminder that national interests cannot justify turning a blind eye to mass atrocities. The world must remember Rwanda as a lesson in the dangers of inaction and a call to uphold the principles of humanity, even in the face of political complexity.

References

- Dallaire, Roméo. *Shake Hands with the Devil: The Failure of Humanity in Rwanda*. Random House Canada, 2003.
- Des Forges, Alison. *Leave None to Tell the Story: Genocide in Rwanda*. Human Rights Watch, 1999.
- Gourevitch, Philip. *We Wish to Inform You That Tomorrow We Will Be Killed with Our Families: Stories from Rwanda*. Picador, 1998.
- Kuperman, Alan. *The Limits of Humanitarian Intervention: Genocide in Rwanda*. Brookings Institution Press, 2001.
- Mamdani, Mahmood. *When Victims Become Killers: Colonialism, Nativism, and the Genocide in Rwanda*. Princeton University Press, 2001.
- Melvern, Linda. *A People Betrayed: The Role of the West in Rwanda's Genocide*. Zed Books, 2000.
- Power, Samantha. *A Problem from Hell: America and the Age of Genocide*. Basic Books, 2002.

- Prunier, Gérard. *The Rwanda Crisis: History of a Genocide*. Columbia University Press, 1995.

6

Power Politics and the Ethics of Non-Intervention

The Rwandan genocide highlighted a profound moral and political dilemma that has long plagued the international community: the tension between respecting state sovereignty and upholding the responsibility to protect human rights. In Rwanda, the prioritization of state sovereignty and political interests over humanitarian intervention allowed the genocide to continue unchecked, leading to the deaths of nearly one million people. This chapter examines the ethical considerations and political factors that influenced the decision-making of major powers, the United Nations, and other actors during the genocide. It analyzes the reasons behind their reluctance to intervene and explores the lessons learned in terms of balancing national interests with the ethical imperative to protect human life.

The Doctrine of State Sovereignty vs. Humanitarian Responsibility

The principle of state sovereignty is a cornerstone of international law, enshrined in the United Nations Charter and respected by most states as a safeguard against external interference. Sovereignty implies that a state has the right to control its internal affairs without foreign intervention. However, when a state fails to protect its citizens from genocide, crimes against humanity, or other mass atrocities, this principle can come into conflict with the ethical imperative to intervene.

Samantha Power, in her book *A Problem from Hell: America and the Age of Genocide*, discusses the dilemma posed by state sovereignty during the Rwandan genocide: "The respect for sovereignty often eclipsed the moral imperative to intervene, as the world chose to look away from Rwanda under the guise of non-interference" (Power, 2002,

p. 421). The reluctance to violate Rwanda's sovereignty, despite the mounting evidence of genocide, exemplifies the prioritization of legal principles over ethical obligations.

The concept of humanitarian intervention, which advocates for intervention in cases of severe human rights abuses, was widely debated during the Rwandan genocide. Mahmood Mamdani argues that the genocide in Rwanda exposed the limitations of sovereignty when human rights are at stake: "Rwanda forced the world to re-examine the principle of sovereignty, as it became clear that non-intervention was a form of complicity in the face of mass murder" (Mamdani, 2001, p. 320). The events in Rwanda would later fuel discussions on the Responsibility to Protect (R2P), a principle that emerged in response to the failure to prevent atrocities like the Rwandan genocide.

The Influence of National Interests

During the Rwandan genocide, key international actors, including the United States, France, and Belgium, prioritized their own national interests over humanitarian concerns. Fear of political backlash, loss of soldiers, and entanglement in an African conflict all influenced these countries' reluctance to take meaningful action.

The United States' stance was heavily influenced by the failure of a peacekeeping mission in Somalia the previous year, where American soldiers were killed in a highly publicized incident. This event led to a cautious approach toward African interventions. Power writes, "The 'Somalia Syndrome' paralyzed the United States, as policymakers feared that any intervention in Rwanda could lead to another costly and politically damaging debacle" (Power, 2002, p. 376). Internal documents reveal that U.S. officials were instructed to avoid using the term "genocide" to evade any legal obligation to intervene, highlighting a calculated decision to sidestep moral responsibilities.

Similarly, France's involvement in Rwanda was motivated by geopolitical interests. France had a close relationship with President Habyarimana's government and viewed Rwanda as a strategic ally in the Francophone world. Gérard Prunier explains, "France saw its influence in Rwanda as a way to counterbalance Anglo-American influence in the region. This alliance led France to support Habyarimana's regime, even as evidence of mass killing emerged" (Prunier, 1995, p. 185). When the genocide began, France's intervention through *Opération Turquoise* was criticized for protecting Hutu extremists rather than stopping the massacres, reflecting France's prioritization of its own strategic interests.

The Role of Bureaucratic Inertia and Institutional Limitations

The United Nations, despite being the institution best positioned to prevent or halt the genocide, was hamstrung by its own bureaucratic structure and institutional limitations. UNAMIR, the United Nations Assistance Mission for Rwanda, was initially deployed to oversee the peace process between the Rwandan government and the RPF. However, when the genocide began, UNAMIR's mandate did not allow for forceful intervention to protect civilians, and requests for additional troops and resources were denied.

Roméo Dallaire, the head of UNAMIR, repeatedly warned UN headquarters of the potential for mass violence. In January 1994, Dallaire sent a detailed "genocide fax" to UN officials, outlining plans for mass killings by Hutu extremists. His request for reinforcements and permission to seize weapons stockpiles went unheeded. Dallaire later recounted his frustration, writing, "We had clear evidence that a genocide was being planned, but the UN's bureaucratic machinery and the lack of political will paralyzed any meaningful response" (Dallaire, 2003, p. 145).

The UN's failure to act decisively was compounded by the reluctance of Security Council members to support an intervention in Rwanda. Scott Straus argues, "The UN's response to Rwanda was hindered by institutional limitations and the unwillingness of its most powerful members to risk their own interests" (Straus, 2006, p. 153). The political calculations of these member states ultimately outweighed the moral obligation to intervene, allowing the genocide to proceed unchallenged.

The Moral Dilemma: To Intervene or Not to Intervene

The international community's failure to intervene in Rwanda has prompted intense ethical debate about the moral responsibilities of states in cases of mass atrocity. Many scholars and human rights advocates argue that non-intervention in the face of genocide constitutes a form of moral complicity. Linda Melvern contends, "By failing to act, the international community implicitly sanctioned the genocide, becoming accomplices in one of the darkest episodes of the 20th century" (Melvern, 2000, p. 276).

The ethical question of intervention revolves around balancing respect for state sovereignty with the responsibility to protect human life. While intervention poses risks, the failure to prevent genocide carries an equally heavy moral cost. Philip Gourevitch, who documented the genocide's horrors, reflects on this dilemma: "The choice to do nothing in Rwanda was not a neutral act; it was a decision that allowed hundreds of thousands to perish" (Gourevitch, 1998, p. 254). Gourevitch's words emphasize that inaction in the face of genocide is itself an ethical choice with devastating consequences.

The Emergence of the Responsibility to Protect (R2P)

The genocide in Rwanda and the subsequent international soul-searching contributed to the development of the Responsibility to Protect (R2P) doctrine. R2P, introduced in the early 2000s, posits that states have an obligation to protect their populations from genocide, war crimes, ethnic cleansing, and crimes against humanity. If a state fails to fulfill this duty, the international community has a moral obligation to intervene.

Mahmood Mamdani argues that R2P reflects a necessary shift in the understanding of sovereignty: "R2P redefines sovereignty as a responsibility rather than an absolute right, prioritizing the protection of citizens over the autonomy of states" (Mamdani, 2001, p. 336). The concept of R2P thus represents an attempt to prevent future genocides by reconciling the tension between state sovereignty and human rights.

However, R2P remains controversial and has been inconsistently applied. Critics argue that it is susceptible to misuse for political purposes, while others worry about the challenges of enforcing it effectively. Samantha Power notes, "R2P offers a framework for intervention, but without the political will to act, it risks becoming yet another hollow promise" (Power, 2002, p. 450). The Rwandan genocide thus serves as both a catalyst and a cautionary tale in the debate over R2P, highlighting the potential and limitations of humanitarian intervention.

Learning from Rwanda: Ethical and Practical Lessons

The Rwandan genocide forced the international community to confront its failures and rethink its approach to preventing mass atrocities. One key lesson is the need for early warning systems and a proactive approach to identifying and addressing signs of impending genocide. Alison Des Forges emphasizes the importance of timely action, writing, "Had the international community responded to the warning signs, many lives could have been saved. The tragedy of Rwanda was not that it was unexpected, but that it was ignored" (Des Forges, 1999, p. 342).

Another lesson is the necessity of a clear and flexible mandate for peacekeeping missions. UNAMIR's limited mandate prevented it from protecting civilians, revealing the limitations of traditional peacekeeping in situations of mass violence. Roméo Dallaire advocates for stronger peacekeeping mandates, arguing, "In cases of genocide, peacekeepers must be empowered to act decisively to protect civilians. A mandate to observe is insufficient when lives are on the line" (Dallaire, 2003, p. 298).

The failure in Rwanda also underscores the need for political will among powerful nations. The reluctance of the United States, France, and other countries to intervene reveals the importance of aligning national interests with humanitarian principles. Linda Melvern argues, "Without the commitment of powerful nations, any framework for intervention remains ineffectual" (Melvern, 2000, p. 301). This lesson remains relevant today, as the world grapples with ongoing crises that demand both ethical leadership and political courage.

Conclusion: The High Cost of Non-Intervention

The Rwandan genocide is a stark reminder of the ethical cost of inaction. The reluctance of the international community to intervene, driven by political considerations, respect for state sovereignty, and bureaucratic inertia, resulted in unimaginable suffering. The legacy of Rwanda is a powerful indictment of a world that prioritized political expediency over human rights.

As Scott Straus concludes, "The genocide in Rwanda was a test of the world's commitment to human rights, and it failed spectacularly" (Straus, 2006, p. 165). The lessons of Rwanda continue to resonate, shaping the debate on intervention, sovereignty, and the responsibility to protect. The ethical imperative to act in the face of mass atrocity remains as pressing as ever, reminding us that true respect for humanity requires the courage to transcend political boundaries and uphold the universal right to life.

References

- Dallaire, Roméo. *Shake Hands with the Devil: The Failure of Humanity in Rwanda*. Random House Canada, 2003.
- Des Forges, Alison. *Leave None to Tell the Story: Genocide in Rwanda*. Human Rights Watch, 1999.
- Gourevitch, Philip. *We Wish to Inform You That Tomorrow We Will Be Killed with Our Families: Stories from Rwanda*. Picador, 1998.
- Mamdani, Mahmood. *When Victims Become Killers: Colonialism, Nativism, and the Genocide in Rwanda*. Princeton University Press, 2001.
- Melvern, Linda. *A People Betrayed: The Role of the West in Rwanda's Genocide*. Zed Books, 2000.
- Power, Samantha. *A Problem from Hell: America and the Age of Genocide*. Basic Books, 2002.
- Prunier, Gérard. *The Rwanda Crisis: History of a Genocide*. Columbia University Press, 1995.
- Straus, Scott. *The Order of Genocide: Race, Power, and War in Rwanda*. Cornell University Press, 2006.

Part III: Aftermath and Rebuilding Rwanda

7

After the Genocide – A Broken Nation Rebuilds

After the genocide ended in July 1994 with the defeat of the genocidal Hutu government by the Rwandan Patriotic Front (RPF), Rwanda faced an almost unimaginable task: to rebuild a society shattered by violence, trauma, and distrust. The genocide left Rwanda in ruins—physically, economically, and emotionally. The new RPF-led government, under the leadership of Paul Kagame, embarked on an ambitious path of recovery, emphasizing justice, reconciliation, and national unity. This chapter examines Rwanda's efforts to rebuild in the aftermath of the genocide, highlighting the challenges of achieving justice, addressing the trauma endured by survivors, and creating a new national identity grounded in unity rather than division.

The Human and Social Toll of Genocide

The impact of the genocide on Rwandan society was profound. Nearly one million people—approximately 10% of the population—were killed, and countless others were left traumatized, widowed, orphaned, or disabled. Families were torn apart, communities shattered, and survivors faced the dual burdens of mourning lost loved ones and coping with the horrors they had endured.

Philip Gourevitch, in his seminal work *We Wish to Inform You That Tomorrow We Will Be Killed with Our Families*, captures the emotional devastation left in the wake of the genocide: "Rwanda was a nation haunted by ghosts, where every person was both a survivor and a witness to unspeakable horrors" (Gourevitch, 1998, p. 221). The sheer scale of loss created a pervasive sense of despair and left many questioning how a society could heal from such atrocities.

The genocide also deeply damaged the social fabric of Rwanda, as neighbors had turned against neighbors, and communities had been torn apart by violence. Scott Straus notes, "The genocide left behind an almost unbridgeable divide, as survivors struggled to live among those who had participated in the massacres" (Straus, 2006, p. 145). Rebuilding this fractured society required a delicate balance of justice and reconciliation, along with an acknowledgment of the trauma experienced by both victims and perpetrators.

Justice for Genocide: The ICTR and the Gacaca Courts

Achieving justice for the genocide was one of the most challenging and essential aspects of Rwanda's recovery. The sheer number of perpetrators, combined with the logistical and moral challenges of prosecuting genocide, required innovative approaches to justice. Two primary systems were established to address the crimes committed during the genocide: the International Criminal Tribunal for Rwanda (ICTR) and the Gacaca Courts.

The ICTR

The International Criminal Tribunal for Rwanda (ICTR) was established by the United Nations Security Council in November 1994 with the mandate to prosecute high-ranking individuals responsible for the genocide and other violations of international law. Based in Arusha, Tanzania, the ICTR sought to bring those most responsible to justice and set a precedent for accountability in cases of genocide. As Alison Des Forges notes, "The ICTR was an important step toward international justice, but it faced numerous challenges, including limited resources, slow proceedings, and difficulty capturing key suspects" (Des Forges, 1999, p. 367).

While the ICTR succeeded in prosecuting several high-ranking officials, including former Prime Minister Jean Kambanda, critics argue that it was too remote from the people of Rwanda and too slow to address the needs of survivors. Mahmood Mamdani points out that "the ICTR was largely removed from the communities most affected by the genocide, making it difficult for ordinary Rwandans to feel connected to the justice process" (Mamdani, 2001, p. 345). Nevertheless, the ICTR contributed to the development of international jurisprudence on genocide, setting a legal standard that would influence future cases of mass atrocity.

The Gacaca Courts

Recognizing the limitations of the ICTR and the overwhelming number of cases to address, the Rwandan government revived a traditional form of community justice known as *Gacaca* (meaning "grass" in Kinyarwanda, symbolizing gathering on the grass to resolve disputes). The Gacaca courts were designed to handle the vast number of low-level genocide cases and to provide a means for local communities to achieve justice and reconciliation.

The Gacaca courts, which began operating in 2001, allowed for a community-based approach to justice, where local judges, known as *inyangamugayo* ("persons of integrity"), heard cases and allowed both perpetrators and survivors to testify. Linda Melvern writes, "The Gacaca courts were an attempt to reconcile justice with the practical need to reintegrate perpetrators into society while providing a forum for survivors to share their stories" (Melvern, 2000, p. 312).

The Gacaca system had its critics, with some arguing that it lacked due process protections and risked exacerbating tensions. However, the courts played a crucial role in allowing Rwandans to confront the past and find a path toward reconciliation. Scott Straus reflects on the Gacaca's impact, noting, "While imperfect, Gacaca provided a means for Rwandans to address the past in a way that was accessible and relevant to local communities" (Straus, 2006, p. 179).

Addressing Trauma and Rebuilding Lives

The psychological impact of the genocide on survivors was immense. Many experienced symptoms of post-traumatic stress disorder (PTSD), depression, and anxiety. The Rwandan government and various non-governmental organizations (NGOs) have worked to provide mental health support to survivors, though resources remain limited. Roméo Dallaire, in *Shake Hands with the Devil*, highlights the long-term effects of trauma on survivors: "The genocide inflicted wounds that were both physical and psychological. The scars left on the minds of survivors will take generations to heal" (Dallaire, 2003, p. 332).

Programs aimed at trauma healing and reconciliation, such as group therapy sessions and support networks for widows and orphans, have been implemented to help survivors cope with their experiences. Philip Gourevitch describes these efforts as a testament to the resilience of the Rwandan people: "In the face of unimaginable suffering, survivors have found ways to rebuild their lives, drawing strength from each other and from their determination to overcome the past" (Gourevitch, 1998, p. 242).

However, challenges remain. Many survivors continue to live in close proximity to those who participated in the genocide, creating an environment of tension and fear. Efforts to promote unity and reconciliation are ongoing, but the trauma inflicted by the genocide remains deeply embedded in Rwandan society.

Forging a New National Identity: Unity Over Division

One of the most remarkable aspects of Rwanda's post-genocide recovery has been the government's focus on forging a national identity that transcends ethnic divisions. The RPF-led government, under the leadership of Paul Kagame, has promoted a vision of "Rwandanness" that emphasizes unity over ethnic identity. Ethnic labels such as "Hutu" and "Tutsi" have been discouraged in official discourse, with the government promoting a message that all Rwandans are equal members of a single national community.

Mahmood Mamdani reflects on this shift, stating, "The new Rwandan identity promoted by the government represents a deliberate attempt to break from the past and redefine the social fabric of the nation" (Mamdani, 2001, p. 351). This approach, while controversial, aims to create a society where ethnic distinctions are less significant than a shared commitment to national progress and unity.

Critics argue that suppressing ethnic identities risks ignoring the historical realities that contributed to the genocide. However, proponents contend that promoting a unified Rwandan identity is essential for long-term peace. As Linda Melvern notes, "Rwanda's emphasis on national unity may be one of its greatest strengths, providing a foundation for stability and growth in a society still haunted by the legacy of division" (Melvern, 2000, p. 336).

Economic and Social Reconstruction

Rebuilding Rwanda's economy was another priority for the post-genocide government. The genocide had devastated Rwanda's infrastructure, leaving schools, hospitals, and roads in ruins. The government launched ambitious development projects aimed at revitalizing the economy, improving education, and reducing poverty. Rwanda has achieved remarkable economic growth, positioning itself as one of Africa's fastest-growing economies and attracting foreign investment.

Stephen Kinzer, in *A Thousand Hills: Rwanda's Rebirth and the Man Who Dreamed It*, documents Rwanda's economic transformation under Kagame's leadership: "Rwanda's focus on development, technology, and infrastructure has turned it into a model of African progress, lifting millions out of poverty and providing hope for a brighter future" (Kinzer, 2008, p. 198). The government has invested heavily in education, healthcare, and technology, aiming to create a knowledge-based economy that can sustain long-term growth.

The government's emphasis on gender equality has also been a key factor in Rwanda's reconstruction. Rwanda now boasts one of the highest rates of female representation in parliament in the world. Alison Des Forges notes, "Rwanda's commitment to empowering women is part of a broader strategy to rebuild a society that values equality and inclusion" (Des Forges, 1999, p. 401).

Challenges and Controversies in Rebuilding Rwanda

While Rwanda's progress has been widely praised, the post-genocide government has also faced criticism. Human rights organizations have raised concerns about restrictions on political freedom, media censorship, and the government's intolerance of dissent. Critics argue that the government's emphasis on stability and unity has sometimes come at the cost of political openness and freedom of expression.

Mahmood Mamdani warns of the potential risks of an authoritarian approach to governance, stating, "Rwanda's success in rebuilding its society cannot be separated from its political context, where freedom of expression and political opposition are limited" (Mamdani, 2001, p. 362). The government's approach to reconciliation has also been criticized for its top-down structure, with some arguing that it does not fully address the needs of local communities.

Despite these challenges, Rwanda's transformation remains an impressive example of resilience and determination. The government has maintained peace and stability in a region historically plagued by conflict, and its development initiatives have significantly improved the quality of life for many Rwandans. Linda Melvern reflects on this achievement, writing, "Rwanda's journey from genocide to growth is a testament to the will of its people and the vision of its leaders" (Melvern, 2000, p. 361).

Conclusion: Resilience and Renewal

Rwanda's post-genocide recovery is a story of resilience, determination, and transformation. The country has navigated the difficult path of justice, reconciliation, and national unity, forging a new identity rooted in peace and progress. While challenges remain, Rwanda's achievements offer a powerful example of a nation that has not only survived but also found a way to thrive.

As Philip Gourevitch observes, "Rwanda's transformation is a testament to the strength of its people, who have refused to be defined by the horrors of the past. They have chosen to rebuild, to forgive, and to create a future where the specter of genocide no longer defines their identity" (Gourevitch, 1998, p. 277). Rwanda's recovery serves as both an inspiration and a reminder that even the most shattered societies can find a path to healing and renewal.

References

- Dallaire, Roméo. *Shake Hands with the Devil: The Failure of Humanity in Rwanda*. Random House Canada, 2003.
- Des Forges, Alison. *Leave None to Tell the Story: Genocide in Rwanda*. Human Rights Watch, 1999.
- Gourevitch, Philip. *We Wish to Inform You That Tomorrow We Will Be Killed with Our Families: Stories from Rwanda*. Picador, 1998.
- Kinzer, Stephen. *A Thousand Hills: Rwanda's Rebirth and the Man Who Dreamed It*. John Wiley & Sons, 2008.
- Mamdani, Mahmood. *When Victims Become Killers: Colonialism, Nativism, and the Genocide in Rwanda*. Princeton University Press, 2001.
- Melvern, Linda. *A People Betrayed: The Role of the West in Rwanda's*

Genocide. Zed Books, 2000.
- Straus, Scott. *The Order of Genocide: Race, Power, and War in Rwanda.* Cornell University Press, 2006.

8

Justice for Genocide – The ICTR and Gacaca Courts

After the genocide ended in Rwanda in 1994, justice became a critical component of the country's path to recovery. Achieving justice was essential not only for punishing perpetrators but also for helping survivors find a sense of closure and for fostering a society based on accountability and reconciliation. Given the enormous scale of the genocide and the vast number of perpetrators, Rwanda faced unique challenges in its pursuit of justice. This chapter examines the dual justice systems that emerged in the aftermath of the genocide: the International Criminal Tribunal for Rwanda (ICTR) and the Gacaca Courts. Each system had its strengths and limitations, and together, they reflected Rwanda's complex needs for justice, accountability, and community healing.

The International Criminal Tribunal for Rwanda (ICTR)

Establishment and Mandate

In November 1994, the United Nations Security Council established the International Criminal Tribunal for Rwanda (ICTR), based in Arusha, Tanzania. The ICTR's mandate was to prosecute high-ranking officials responsible for planning and executing the genocide, as well as other serious violations of international law. The tribunal aimed to bring the principal architects of the genocide to justice and to set a legal precedent for prosecuting mass atrocity crimes.

Alison Des Forges described the ICTR as "an important step toward international accountability, representing a commitment by the world community to pursue justice in the face of unimaginable crimes" (Des Forges, 1999, p. 382). However, the ICTR faced significant challenges, including a limited budget, bureaucratic delays, and difficulties in apprehending suspects. The tribunal initially struggled to establish credibility among the Rwandan people, many of whom felt disconnected from the distant court proceedings in Arusha.

Major Achievements of the ICTR

Despite its limitations, the ICTR accomplished several important milestones. One of its most notable successes was the prosecution of Jean Kambanda, the former Prime Minister of Rwanda, who became the first head of government to be convicted of genocide. Kambanda's conviction sent a powerful message about accountability, establishing that even political leaders could be held responsible for atrocities. In total, the ICTR indicted 93 individuals, securing convictions for high-ranking military leaders, government officials, and media figures responsible for inciting genocide.

Philip Gourevitch highlighted the significance of these convictions, noting, "The ICTR's work showed that justice could reach even those at the highest levels of power, marking a critical step in the international community's response to genocide" (Gourevitch, 1998, p. 254). The ICTR's verdicts helped to develop international jurisprudence on genocide, particularly regarding the prosecution of incitement to genocide, and contributed to the evolving understanding of crimes against humanity and war crimes.

Criticisms and Limitations of the ICTR

While the ICTR played a crucial role in bringing high-level perpetrators to justice, it was also widely criticized for its slow pace, high costs, and lack of local engagement. The tribunal operated for nearly two decades, and its lengthy proceedings frustrated many Rwandans, who saw it as removed from their everyday reality. Scott Straus argues, "The ICTR's detachment from the local context limited its impact on Rwandan society and created a gap between international justice and the needs of the people most affected by the genocide" (Straus, 2006, p. 201).

The ICTR also faced criticism for failing to prosecute members of the Rwandan Patriotic Front (RPF) for alleged war crimes committed during and after the genocide. This omission led some to accuse the tribunal of biased justice, as it prosecuted only one side of the conflict. Mahmood Mamdani observes, "The ICTR's exclusive focus on the Hutu perpetrators raised questions about the impartiality of international justice and highlighted the complexities of achieving justice in a post-genocide context" (Mamdani, 2001, p. 357).

Despite these criticisms, the ICTR's legacy endures as a landmark in international criminal justice. Its work established important legal precedents, raised awareness of genocide as a prosecutable crime, and set the stage for future international tribunals, including those for the former Yugoslavia, Sierra Leone, and Cambodia.

The Gacaca Courts: Community-Based Justice

Origins and Objectives of Gacaca

In addition to the ICTR, the Rwandan government recognized the need for a justice mechanism that could address the vast number of low-level perpetrators while also promoting community healing. The Gacaca courts, a traditional form of community justice, were revived and adapted to meet this challenge. In 2001, the Gacaca system was implemented nationwide, with the goal of handling cases related to genocide, promoting truth-telling, fostering reconciliation, and reintegrating perpetrators into society.

Linda Melvern describes Gacaca as "a bold experiment in justice, aiming to achieve accountability and healing at the grassroots level" (Melvern, 2000, p. 345). Unlike the ICTR, which focused on high-level officials, the Gacaca courts targeted low-level perpetrators—individuals who had participated in killings, looting, or other acts of violence but were not considered the masterminds of the genocide.

Structure and Function of Gacaca Courts

The Gacaca system operated on a community level, with local judges, known as *inyangamugayo* (persons of integrity), presiding over cases in open-air gatherings. Both survivors and accused perpetrators were encouraged to testify, allowing communities to confront the truth of what had occurred. The process was designed to encourage confessions, repentance, and forgiveness, with the hope that survivors and perpetrators could coexist peacefully in the same communities.

Scott Straus notes, "The Gacaca courts represented a unique approach to justice, emphasizing restorative principles over punitive measures, and seeking to rebuild social cohesion in a deeply divided society" (Straus, 2006, p. 215). By involving communities directly in the justice process, Gacaca sought to make justice accessible and relevant to ordinary Rwandans.

Achievements of Gacaca

The Gacaca courts handled an estimated 1.2 million cases between 2001 and 2012, making it one of the most extensive judicial processes in history. Through Gacaca, countless perpetrators were held accountable, and many survivors were able to learn the fate of their loved ones. The Gacaca courts allowed Rwandan society to confront the truth and fostered a culture of accountability at the grassroots level.

Alison Des Forges acknowledges the impact of Gacaca, stating, "Despite its flaws, Gacaca gave survivors a voice, helped heal communities, and allowed Rwandans to reclaim a sense of justice" (Des Forges, 1999, p. 403). The system played an essential role in Rwanda's recovery by enabling communities to come to terms with the past, promoting reconciliation, and facilitating the reintegration of lower-level perpetrators.

Criticisms and Limitations of Gacaca

While the Gacaca courts achieved many of their objectives, they also faced significant criticisms. Human rights organizations raised concerns about the lack of due process in Gacaca, as defendants were often denied legal representation, and the judges lacked formal legal training. Furthermore, the open nature of Gacaca hearings sometimes exposed survivors to intimidation and re-traumatization.

Mahmood Mamdani highlights these challenges, arguing, "The Gacaca courts sacrificed some elements of due process in favor of expediency, creating a tension between the desire for justice and the practical realities of Rwanda's post-genocide context" (Mamdani, 2001, p. 364). The courts also faced accusations of bias, with some survivors feeling that certain perpetrators received lenient sentences, while others viewed the process as overly harsh on lower-level participants who acted under coercion.

Another significant critique was that Gacaca focused predominantly on Hutu perpetrators, while crimes committed by the RPF went largely unaddressed. This selective justice led to perceptions of partiality, potentially undermining Gacaca's credibility in some communities. Linda Melvern notes, "The perception of one-sided justice remains a challenge for Rwanda, as Gacaca's focus on Hutu perpetrators left unanswered questions about RPF accountability" (Melvern, 2000, p. 358).

Justice and Reconciliation: Balancing Accountability and Healing

The dual justice systems of the ICTR and Gacaca reflect Rwanda's efforts to balance accountability with the need for reconciliation and healing. The ICTR's focus on high-ranking officials and international law provided a model for prosecuting genocide, while the Gacaca courts allowed Rwandans to engage directly with the process of justice in their communities.

The Gacaca system, despite its limitations, embodied a restorative approach to justice, emphasizing reconciliation over retribution. Philip Gourevitch observes, "The Gacaca courts allowed Rwandans to confront their past, seeking not only punishment but also forgiveness and understanding" (Gourevitch, 1998, p. 291). This approach was critical in a society where survivors and perpetrators would need to live side by side for years to come.

Roméo Dallaire, who witnessed the horrors of the genocide firsthand, reflected on Rwanda's pursuit of justice, stating, "Rwanda's path to justice was imperfect, but it demonstrated a commitment to confronting the truth and rebuilding trust in a shattered nation" (Dallaire, 2003, p. 349). The combination of the ICTR and Gacaca courts provided complementary avenues for justice, addressing both the highest levels of responsibility and the needs of local communities.

Legacy and Lessons for International Justice

The experiences of the ICTR and Gacaca have left a lasting impact on international and community-based approaches to justice. The ICTR contributed to the development of international criminal law and established precedents that continue to shape tribunals worldwide. Its achievements, as well as its shortcomings, have informed the structure and procedures of subsequent international courts.

The Gacaca system, meanwhile, has influenced thinking on transitional justice by demonstrating how traditional mechanisms can be adapted to address large-scale atrocities. Scott Straus emphasizes, "Gacaca's innovations in community justice have broadened the scope of transitional justice, illustrating that accountability can take many forms beyond the conventional courtroom" (Straus, 2006, p. 230).

However, the Rwandan experience also underscores the complexities and limitations of justice in post-genocide societies. Mahmood Mamdani reflects, "The Rwandan case demonstrates that justice is a multifaceted endeavor, and that in the wake of mass atrocity, societies must balance the demands of punishment, reconciliation, and social healing" (Mamdani, 2001, p. 372). The lessons of Rwanda remind the international community of the importance of adapting justice mechanisms to the specific needs and contexts of affected societies.

Conclusion: Justice as a Path to Reconciliation

The ICTR and Gacaca courts together represent Rwanda's multifaceted approach to justice after the genocide. While neither system was perfect, each played a vital role in addressing the legacy of violence and fostering a sense of accountability. The ICTR established an international precedent, while Gacaca engaged communities directly, allowing Rwandans to confront their painful history.

As Linda Melvern concludes, "The pursuit of justice in Rwanda was not without flaws, but it was essential for healing a nation scarred by violence. Rwanda's willingness to pursue both international and community-based justice offers a model for post-conflict societies worldwide" (Melvern, 2000, p. 372). The ICTR and Gacaca reflect Rwanda's resilience and determination to rebuild, demonstrating that justice, even when imperfect, is a critical step on the path to reconciliation.

References

- Dallaire, Roméo. *Shake Hands with the Devil: The Failure of Humanity in Rwanda*. Random House Canada, 2003.
- Des Forges, Alison. *Leave None to Tell the Story: Genocide in Rwanda*. Human Rights Watch, 1999.
- Gourevitch, Philip. *We Wish to Inform You That Tomorrow We Will Be Killed with Our Families: Stories from Rwanda*. Picador, 1998.
- Mamdani, Mahmood. *When Victims Become Killers: Colonialism, Nativism, and the Genocide in Rwanda*. Princeton University Press, 2001.
- Melvern, Linda. *A People Betrayed: The Role of the West in Rwanda's Genocide*. Zed Books, 2000.

- Straus, Scott. *The Order of Genocide: Race, Power, and War in Rwanda.* Cornell University Press, 2006.

9

From Ashes to Ascendancy – Rwanda's Remarkable Rebirth

In the aftermath of the genocide, Rwanda faced an extraordinary challenge: to rebuild a society ravaged by violence, division, and trauma. The scale of the destruction left in the genocide's wake was almost incomprehensible, yet in the decades that followed, Rwanda emerged as one of Africa's most stable and rapidly developing nations. Under the leadership of the Rwandan Patriotic Front (RPF) and President Paul Kagame, Rwanda has undergone a remarkable transformation, focusing on economic growth, social cohesion, and political stability. This chapter examines Rwanda's journey of rebirth, exploring the policies and reforms that propelled its development, the successes achieved, and the controversies that accompany its progress.

The Vision of a New Rwanda

The vision for a new Rwanda, spearheaded by the RPF government, was rooted in the ideals of unity, reconciliation, and socioeconomic progress. Kagame and the RPF's primary goal was to create a society where ethnicity would no longer define individuals, and Rwandans could move forward with a shared national identity.

Mahmood Mamdani reflects on this shift in identity, stating, "Rwanda's post-genocide leadership aimed to redefine what it means to be Rwandan, erasing ethnic divisions in favor of a collective national identity" (Mamdani, 2001, p. 380). This focus on unity was not only a response to the genocide but also a strategy to prevent future violence by eliminating the factors that had historically fueled division.

The government introduced a policy of "Ndi Umunyarwanda" ("I am Rwandan"), which discouraged ethnic classifications and promoted national unity. This policy was embedded in education, media, and public discourse. Linda Melvern observes, "By promoting a common Rwandan identity, the government sought to build a cohesive society where divisions of the past would not dictate the future" (Melvern, 2000, p. 382).

While the "Ndi Umunyarwanda" policy has been largely successful in fostering unity, some critics argue that it suppresses legitimate expressions of identity and stifles public discussion of ethnicity. Philip Gourevitch notes, "In Rwanda, ethnicity has become a taboo topic, a strategy that has prevented open dialogue but has also preserved peace in a fragile society" (Gourevitch, 1998, p. 301).

Economic Transformation and Development

Rwanda's economic growth in the post-genocide years has been nothing short of remarkable. The government embarked on an ambitious development agenda, focused on transforming Rwanda into a middle-income country. This vision, known as "Vision 2020" and later "Vision 2050," sought to turn Rwanda into a knowledge-based economy, reduce poverty, and improve infrastructure and public services.

Stephen Kinzer, in his book *A Thousand Hills: Rwanda's Rebirth and the Man Who Dreamed It*, describes Rwanda's economic transformation as "one of the most ambitious and disciplined development agendas in Africa, with a relentless focus on modernization and efficiency" (Kinzer, 2008, p. 178). Under Vision 2020, Rwanda made significant investments in education, healthcare, infrastructure, and technology. The government encouraged foreign investment, established special economic zones, and prioritized sectors such as information technology and tourism.

Rwanda's commitment to gender equality has also contributed to its economic success. Today, Rwanda has one of the highest percentages of women in parliament globally, and women play a vital role in the country's workforce. Alison Des Forges notes, "The empowerment of women has been a cornerstone of Rwanda's recovery, with women leading in sectors ranging from politics to agriculture" (Des Forges, 1999, p. 411).

One of the most striking examples of Rwanda's economic transformation is its capital, Kigali, which has become a symbol of the country's progress. Known for its cleanliness, safety, and modern infrastructure, Kigali represents Rwanda's aspiration to redefine itself on the world stage. However, this transformation has come with significant costs, including allegations of forced relocations and displacement of low-income residents. Mamdani remarks, "While Rwanda's development model is impressive, it is not without its controversies, as rapid urbanization has led to questions about inclusivity and equity" (Mamdani, 2001, p. 395).

Healthcare and Education Reforms

Rwanda's progress in healthcare and education has been pivotal to its development. In the healthcare sector, Rwanda has implemented innovative programs that have drastically improved public health outcomes. The government invested in community-based healthcare, focusing on preventive care and maternal health. By training community health workers and improving access to healthcare services, Rwanda has achieved significant reductions in child mortality and infectious diseases.

Roméo Dallaire commends Rwanda's health reforms, writing, "Rwanda's healthcare system is a model of innovation, demonstrating how a country can rebuild its health infrastructure from the ground up" (Dallaire, 2003, p. 371). Programs such as Mutuelles de Santé, a community-based health insurance scheme, have improved healthcare accessibility, with over 90% of Rwandans now covered by health insurance.

Education has also been a priority, with the government emphasizing both primary education and higher education as part of its strategy to create a knowledge-based economy. The introduction of free primary education, investments in vocational training, and partnerships with international universities have all contributed to the rapid expansion of Rwanda's education sector. Kinzer observes, "Rwanda's emphasis on education is central to its development vision, as the government seeks to cultivate a generation equipped with skills for a modern economy" (Kinzer, 2008, p. 204).

Social Reconciliation and Unity

Reconciliation has been a cornerstone of Rwanda's rebuilding efforts. Recognizing that sustainable peace required addressing the trauma and distrust caused by the genocide, the Rwandan government implemented a range of programs aimed at fostering reconciliation. These included the Gacaca courts, which allowed communities to confront their past, and initiatives that promote dialogue and forgiveness.

The establishment of memorials, such as the Kigali Genocide Memorial, serves as a reminder of the past and a testament to Rwanda's commitment to honoring the memory of genocide victims. Scott Straus notes, "Memorialization is an essential part of Rwanda's journey of reconciliation, providing spaces where Rwandans can mourn together and renew their commitment to peace" (Straus, 2006, p. 241).

However, some critics argue that the government's approach to reconciliation is top-down and suppresses open discussion about ethnic identity and historical grievances. Mamdani points out, "The government's emphasis on unity sometimes glosses over the complexities of reconciliation, as Rwandans are expected to move forward without fully addressing underlying issues" (Mamdani, 2001, p. 413). While Rwanda's model has succeeded in maintaining stability, questions about freedom of expression and the government's control over historical narratives remain.

Controversies and Criticisms of Governance

Despite Rwanda's impressive achievements, the Kagame administration has faced criticism for its governance practices. Human rights organizations have raised concerns about restrictions on political freedom, media censorship, and the suppression of opposition voices. The government's tight control over public discourse and its intolerance of dissent have sparked debate about the trade-off between stability and political openness.

Alison Des Forges warns, "Rwanda's approach to governance, while effective in maintaining order, risks silencing legitimate dissent and curbing political freedom" (Des Forges, 1999, p. 432). The government's commitment to stability has sometimes been viewed as authoritarian, with accusations of harassment and imprisonment of political opponents.

Samantha Power also addresses this tension, noting, "Rwanda's achievements cannot be overlooked, but neither can the constraints on political freedom, which challenge the narrative of a fully democratic society" (Power, 2002, p. 478). While Kagame's leadership has been pivotal in driving Rwanda's development, the balance between state control and individual freedoms remains a topic of international concern.

Rwanda's Role on the Global Stage

Rwanda has positioned itself as a leader in African development and as a model for post-conflict recovery. The country has actively participated in peacekeeping missions across Africa, contributing troops to UN missions in Sudan, South Sudan, and the Central African Republic. Kagame's government has sought to promote Rwanda as an example of African resilience and autonomy, often challenging Western notions of aid and development.

Linda Melvern highlights Rwanda's assertive stance on the global stage, stating, "Rwanda has defied traditional development paradigms, advocating for African solutions to African problems and positioning itself as a regional leader" (Melvern, 2000, p. 412). This assertiveness reflects Rwanda's desire to control its own narrative and development trajectory, rejecting dependency on Western aid and emphasizing self-reliance.

However, Rwanda's involvement in regional politics has not been without controversy. The government has faced accusations of supporting rebel groups in the Democratic Republic of Congo (DRC), which has led to strained relations with neighboring countries and criticism from the international community. Mahmood Mamdani observes, "Rwanda's actions in the DRC reveal the complexities of its regional influence, as the government balances its domestic achievements with contentious foreign policies" (Mamdani, 2001, p. 428).

The Legacy of Rwanda's Transformation

Rwanda's journey from genocide to growth and stability is a testament to the resilience of its people and the determination of its leadership. While the country's progress has been accompanied by challenges and criticisms, Rwanda's transformation remains one of the most remarkable examples of post-conflict recovery in recent history. The government's focus on unity, economic development, and social reconciliation has redefined Rwanda's identity and offered a model for other nations emerging from conflict.

Philip Gourevitch encapsulates Rwanda's transformation, writing, "Rwanda's rise from the ashes is a story of endurance and hope, a reminder that even the darkest past can be followed by a new dawn" (Gourevitch, 1998, p. 314). The lessons of Rwanda's recovery continue to resonate globally, providing valuable insights into the challenges of rebuilding a society after unimaginable trauma.

As Rwanda looks toward the future, its story remains a complex one, shaped by both achievements and unresolved issues. Linda Melvern reflects, "Rwanda's journey is far from over. The successes are undeniable, but the challenges of maintaining unity, ensuring justice, and balancing governance with freedom persist" (Melvern, 2000, p. 442). Rwanda's transformation, while inspiring, is also a reminder of the ongoing work required to build a society that honors the past, embraces the present, and prepares for the future.

References

- Dallaire, Roméo. *Shake Hands with the Devil: The Failure of Humanity in Rwanda*. Random House Canada, 2003.
- Des Forges, Alison. *Leave None to Tell the Story: Genocide in Rwanda*. Human Rights Watch, 1999.
- Gourevitch, Philip. *We Wish to Inform You That Tomorrow We Will Be Killed with Our Families: Stories from Rwanda*. Picador, 1998.
- Kinzer, Stephen. *A Thousand Hills: Rwanda's Rebirth and the Man Who Dreamed It*. John Wiley & Sons, 2008.
- Mamdani, Mahmood. *When Victims Become Killers: Colonialism, Nativism, and the Genocide in Rwanda*. Princeton University Press, 2001.
- Melvern, Linda. *A People Betrayed: The Role of the West in Rwanda's Genocide*. Zed Books, 2000.
- Power, Samantha. *A Problem from Hell: America and the Age of Genocide*. Basic Books, 2002.
- Straus, Scott. *The Order of Genocide: Race, Power, and War in Rwanda*.

Cornell University Press, 2006.

Part IV: Lessons and Reflections

10

Lessons for the Future – State Sovereignty Versus Human Rights

The Rwandan genocide remains one of the most profound tragedies in modern history, exposing the consequences of unchecked hatred and the failure of the international community to intervene in the face of mass atrocity. The lessons learned from Rwanda have reverberated globally, prompting widespread reflection on the balance between state sovereignty and the protection of human rights. This chapter explores the lessons that Rwanda offers for the future, examining the evolution of the Responsibility to Protect (R2P) doctrine, the challenges of early warning and intervention, and the need for a robust international framework that prioritizes the protection of vulnerable populations over political expediency.

The Doctrine of State Sovereignty and Its Limits

The principle of state sovereignty has been a central tenet of international relations, enshrined in the United Nations Charter and respected by nations as a means of protecting their autonomy and internal affairs. However, the Rwandan genocide revealed the limitations of strict adherence to sovereignty when a government fails to protect—or actively targets—its own citizens. In Rwanda, the world's reluctance to violate state sovereignty in the face of clear genocidal intent highlighted a moral failing that would influence future discussions on humanitarian intervention.

Samantha Power, in *A Problem from Hell: America and the Age of Genocide*, reflects on the tension between sovereignty and intervention: "The international community's respect for Rwanda's sovereignty became a shield behind which mass murder was carried out, showing the moral bankruptcy of a world order that places sovereignty above human life" (Power, 2002, p. 473). The refusal to intervene in Rwanda, justified by respect for sovereignty, underscored the need to reassess the boundaries of state autonomy when human rights are at stake.

This lesson influenced the development of the Responsibility to Protect (R2P) doctrine, which posits that sovereignty is not an absolute right but a responsibility. As Scott Straus observes, "Rwanda forced the world to confront the limitations of sovereignty and recognize that when a state fails to protect its citizens, the international community has a moral obligation to act" (Straus, 2006, p. 272).

The Responsibility to Protect (R2P): An Evolving Framework

The Rwandan genocide, along with the atrocities in Bosnia, directly contributed to the establishment of the Responsibility to Protect (R2P) doctrine, adopted by the United Nations in 2005. R2P asserts that states have a responsibility to protect their populations from genocide, war crimes, ethnic cleansing, and crimes against humanity. If a state fails in this duty, the international community has a responsibility to intervene, using diplomatic, humanitarian, or, as a last resort, military means.

Mahmood Mamdani discusses the importance of R2P as a response to the failures in Rwanda: "The Responsibility to Protect doctrine represents a shift in international norms, redefining sovereignty as a responsibility rather than an absolute right. R2P acknowledges that when a state fails to protect its people, the world cannot remain passive" (Mamdani, 2001, p. 389). R2P reflects an understanding that state sovereignty should not serve as a justification for inaction in the face of mass atrocity.

However, R2P remains controversial, as its application has been inconsistent, and some argue that it could be exploited for political purposes. Linda Melvern highlights this tension, stating, "While R2P offers a framework for intervention, its selective application has raised concerns about its potential misuse by powerful states seeking to further their own interests" (Melvern, 2000, p. 487). The challenge for R2P lies in ensuring that it is used solely as a means of protecting human rights, rather than as a tool for geopolitical gain.

The Importance of Early Warning Systems and Preventive Action

One of the clearest lessons from Rwanda is the critical need for effective early warning systems and preventive measures to address the signs of impending genocide or mass atrocity. Before the genocide began, numerous warning signs—including hate speech, political violence, and weapon stockpiling—were evident. Yet, the international community failed to take these indicators seriously, resulting in a catastrophic delay in response.

Roméo Dallaire, who led the United Nations Assistance Mission for Rwanda (UNAMIR), repeatedly warned UN officials of the potential for genocide. His infamous "genocide fax" in January 1994 detailed the plans of Hutu extremists and requested permission to take preventive action. However, Dallaire's warnings went unheeded. Reflecting on this failure, Dallaire writes, "The tragedy of Rwanda is that it was avoidable. The warning signs were there, but bureaucratic inertia and political indifference prevented us from acting" (Dallaire, 2003, p. 327).

The need for robust early warning mechanisms has become a priority in the field of genocide prevention. Philip Gourevitch emphasizes, "Rwanda's experience shows that early intervention can save lives, but only if there is a willingness to recognize and act on warning signs" (Gourevitch, 1998, p. 287). Today, organizations such as the UN Office on Genocide Prevention and the Responsibility to Protect work to identify and monitor potential crises, though challenges in mobilizing resources and political will persist.

The Role of Political Will and International Cooperation

The failure to intervene in Rwanda highlighted the limitations of international mechanisms when political will is absent. Despite clear evidence of genocide, major powers—including the United States, France, and Belgium—were reluctant to take action, driven by concerns about cost, risks, and national interest. The lack of political will to intervene underscored the difficulty of mobilizing an international response in the absence of direct national interests.

Samantha Power critiques this reluctance, stating, "In Rwanda, the absence of political will translated into a deadly indifference. Leaders prioritized their own interests over the lives of Rwandan civilians, with devastating consequences" (Power, 2002, p. 456). This failure to prioritize human rights over political expediency remains a challenge in global governance, as governments continue to weigh humanitarian needs against national considerations.

The Rwandan genocide demonstrated that international cooperation and commitment are essential for effective intervention. Linda Melvern argues, "Rwanda exposed the weakness of international institutions that lack the power to act decisively without the backing of key member states. True intervention requires both collective resolve and a willingness to transcend national self-interest" (Melvern, 2000, p. 509). The international community's ability to prevent future genocides depends on its capacity to foster genuine cooperation and shared responsibility.

The Role of Media and Public Pressure

The Rwandan genocide also underscored the importance of media and public awareness in shaping the response to humanitarian crises. During the genocide, media coverage was sparse, and few journalists were present on the ground. The lack of information contributed to international apathy, as governments faced little public pressure to respond. In contrast, when atrocities receive widespread media attention, public outrage can drive political leaders to take action.

Alison Des Forges reflects on the impact of media indifference, writing, "The world's ignorance of Rwanda's suffering was a moral failure that allowed the genocide to proceed unchallenged. When the public is unaware, leaders feel no pressure to intervene" (Des Forges, 1999, p. 482). Today, social media and global news networks have transformed the dissemination of information, but challenges remain in mobilizing public pressure for timely intervention.

The lesson from Rwanda is that public awareness can play a critical role in preventing and responding to genocide. Philip Gourevitch notes, "An informed public can hold governments accountable, making it harder for leaders to ignore atrocities" (Gourevitch, 1998, p. 299). The growth of global media has expanded the potential for public pressure, though maintaining attention on protracted crises remains difficult.

Building a Robust International Framework for Intervention

The Rwandan genocide underscored the need for a stronger international framework to prevent and respond to mass atrocities. The UN's limited capacity, combined with the absence of a clear mandate for intervention, rendered it largely ineffective during the crisis. Since then, there have been efforts to improve the UN's capacity for rapid response and to clarify the conditions under which intervention is warranted.

Roméo Dallaire advocates for a more proactive approach, arguing, "The UN needs a mandate that empowers peacekeepers to act decisively in the face of genocide. Observation is not enough; intervention requires both the authority and resources to protect civilians" (Dallaire, 2003, p. 353). The establishment of peacekeeping missions with robust mandates, such as the "protection of civilians" doctrine, has been a step in the right direction, though implementation remains inconsistent.

Scott Straus emphasizes the importance of accountability mechanisms within the UN, stating, "A stronger UN framework is essential, but it must also include checks and balances to ensure that peacekeeping missions are held accountable for their actions—or inactions" (Straus, 2006, p. 292). Developing a reliable framework for intervention is an ongoing challenge, as political dynamics and resource constraints continue to impact the UN's effectiveness.

Lessons in Reconciliation and Social Healing

While the international community's failure to prevent the Rwandan genocide has prompted critical lessons about intervention, Rwanda's own journey of reconciliation offers insights into post-genocide recovery. The Gacaca courts, national unity policies, and commemorative practices all reflect Rwanda's commitment to rebuilding a society that prioritizes peace and cohesion.

Mahmood Mamdani highlights Rwanda's focus on reconciliation, noting, "Rwanda's emphasis on unity and reconciliation serves as a model for post-conflict societies. While the path is fraught with challenges, Rwanda's efforts have shown that healing is possible even after profound trauma" (Mamdani, 2001, p. 432). Rwanda's approach demonstrates the importance of addressing historical grievances and fostering social cohesion, lessons that resonate with other societies emerging from conflict.

However, Rwanda's model has also faced criticism for limiting freedom of expression and controlling narratives about the past. Alison Des Forges cautions, "While unity is essential, Rwanda's restrictions on open dialogue raise questions about the balance between stability and political freedom" (Des Forges, 1999, p. 503). The lessons from

Rwanda's recovery highlight the need for a nuanced approach to reconciliation that values both unity and transparency.

Conclusion: Toward a More Compassionate World Order

The Rwandan genocide remains a powerful reminder of the high cost of inaction in the face of mass atrocity. The lessons learned from Rwanda have spurred important developments in international law, humanitarian intervention, and reconciliation practices. However, the challenges of implementing these lessons continue to test the world's commitment to preventing future genocides.

As Samantha Power writes, "Rwanda serves as a moral indictment of a world that failed to act, but it also offers hope that, armed with these lessons, we can build a more compassionate and responsive international system" (Power, 2002, p. 521). The Responsibility to Protect, early warning mechanisms, and post-conflict reconciliation models represent steps toward a more just world, though these frameworks must be strengthened and consistently applied.

The legacy of Rwanda compels us to reevaluate the role of state sovereignty, prioritize human rights, and ensure that "Never Again" is more than a slogan. As Roméo Dallaire poignantly concludes, "Rwanda was a tragedy that could have been prevented. If we are to honor the victims, we must ensure that the world is prepared to protect the innocent and stand against hate" (Dallaire, 2003, p. 372). The lessons of Rwanda challenge us to act with moral courage and compassion, to create a world where genocide is truly consigned to history.

References

- Dallaire, Roméo. *Shake Hands with the Devil: The Failure of Humanity in Rwanda*. Random House Canada, 2003.

- Des Forges, Alison. *Leave None to Tell the Story: Genocide in Rwanda.* Human Rights Watch, 1999.
- Gourevitch, Philip. *We Wish to Inform You That Tomorrow We Will Be Killed with Our Families: Stories from Rwanda.* Picador, 1998.
- Mamdani, Mahmood. *When Victims Become Killers: Colonialism, Nativism, and the Genocide in Rwanda.* Princeton University Press, 2001.
- Melvern, Linda. *A People Betrayed: The Role of the West in Rwanda's Genocide.* Zed Books, 2000.
- Power, Samantha. *A Problem from Hell: America and the Age of Genocide.* Basic Books, 2002.
- Straus, Scott. *The Order of Genocide: Race, Power, and War in Rwanda.* Cornell University Press, 2006.

11

A Call to Action – Preventing Future Genocides

The legacy of the Rwandan genocide serves as both a tragic reminder of the consequences of global inaction and a call to action for the international community. In the years following the genocide, Rwanda has emerged as a symbol of resilience and recovery, but the shadow of its past continues to highlight the urgency of preventing future atrocities.

This chapter explores the steps that can be taken to prevent future genocides, emphasizing the importance of early intervention, strengthening international legal frameworks, building robust human rights institutions, and fostering global education and awareness. The lessons from Rwanda compel the world to act decisively, and this chapter considers what it means to fulfill the promise of "Never Again."

The Importance of Early Intervention and Preventive Measures

One of the most significant lessons from the Rwandan genocide is the need for early intervention and preventive measures. The international community had numerous warning signs of the impending genocide, including hate speech, rising ethnic tensions, and the militarization of Hutu extremists, but failed to take preventive action. Roméo Dallaire, who led the United Nations Assistance Mission for Rwanda (UNAMIR), sent urgent warnings to the UN headquarters before the genocide began. In his memoir *Shake Hands with the Devil*, Dallaire reflects on the missed opportunities for prevention, stating, "The tragedy of Rwanda was not that it was unforeseen but that it was ignored" (Dallaire, 2003, p. 329).

Early intervention requires robust early warning systems that can detect and respond to signs of potential genocide. The United Nations and various human rights organizations have worked to develop such systems, though challenges remain in mobilizing a timely response. Alison Des Forges emphasizes the need for vigilance, noting, "Rwanda taught us that the cost of ignoring early warning signs can be devastating. Prevention requires both the will to see and the courage to act" (Des Forges, 1999, p. 498). Strengthening these systems and ensuring that they trigger action are essential steps toward effective prevention.

Strengthening the Responsibility to Protect (R2P)

The Responsibility to Protect (R2P) doctrine, adopted by the United Nations in 2005, was directly influenced by the failures in Rwanda and Bosnia. R2P asserts that the international community has a moral obligation to protect populations from genocide, war crimes, ethnic cleansing, and crimes against humanity. If a state fails to protect its citizens or is itself a perpetrator, R2P mandates that the international community should intervene.

Samantha Power describes R2P as "a commitment to act when national governments are unwilling or unable to protect their own citizens from mass atrocities" (Power, 2002, p. 503). R2P represents an evolution in international norms, recognizing that sovereignty cannot be an excuse for inaction in the face of genocide. However, the application of R2P has been inconsistent, and it remains controversial, particularly due to concerns about its potential misuse for political purposes.

Linda Melvern addresses these challenges, writing, "R2P must be strengthened and clarified to prevent its misuse. It should be a tool for genuine humanitarian intervention, not a cover for political agendas" (Melvern, 2000, p. 515). Ensuring that R2P is used responsibly requires clear guidelines, transparency, and accountability. As the international community continues to navigate the complexities of intervention, R2P offers a framework that, if applied consistently, could help prevent future genocides.

Building Robust Human Rights Institutions

The Rwandan genocide underscored the importance of strong, independent human rights institutions that can monitor, report, and respond to violations. National and international human rights organizations play a crucial role in documenting abuses, advocating for victims, and pressuring governments to uphold their obligations under international law. Building and supporting these institutions can help create an environment where human rights are respected, and potential atrocities are identified before they escalate.

Mahmood Mamdani argues, "Human rights institutions provide the checks and balances necessary to prevent the abuses that can lead to mass violence. Without accountability mechanisms, impunity reigns, and atrocities become possible" (Mamdani, 2001, p. 421). The establishment of the International Criminal Court (ICC) and the strengthening of regional human rights bodies, such as the African Court on Human and Peoples' Rights, are steps toward creating a global framework for accountability.

However, these institutions face significant challenges, including resource limitations, political resistance, and jurisdictional constraints. Philip Gourevitch notes, "The effectiveness of human rights institutions depends on both political will and the allocation of adequate resources. Without these, even the best intentions remain unfulfilled" (Gourevitch, 1998, p. 312). Supporting and strengthening human rights institutions at all levels—national, regional, and international—is essential for creating a world where genocide can be effectively prevented.

International Justice and Accountability

The pursuit of justice for genocide is essential not only for punishing perpetrators but also for preventing future atrocities by establishing a deterrent. The establishment of the International Criminal Tribunal for Rwanda (ICTR) marked a significant step in the development of international criminal law. The ICTR prosecuted key figures responsible for orchestrating the Rwandan genocide, setting legal precedents for the prosecution of genocide, crimes against humanity, and war crimes.

Scott Straus highlights the importance of accountability in preventing future violence, stating, "The ICTR's work demonstrated that the international community is willing to hold perpetrators accountable, sending a message that genocide is not tolerated" (Straus, 2006, p. 311). By bringing high-ranking officials to justice, the ICTR helped to establish the principle that leaders are not above the law, reinforcing the idea that accountability is crucial to preventing future atrocities.

However, the ICTR also faced criticism for its limited scope, high costs, and slow proceedings. The establishment of the ICC sought to address some of these issues by providing a permanent court with broader jurisdiction. Linda Melvern observes, "The creation of the ICC represents a commitment to universal justice, but its success depends on the cooperation and support of the international community" (Melvern, 2000, p. 532). Strengthening international justice mechanisms and ensuring the ICC's efficacy and impartiality are essential components of genocide prevention.

Fostering Global Education and Awareness

Education is a powerful tool for preventing genocide, as it can foster understanding, empathy, and respect for human rights. In Rwanda, the government has implemented programs aimed at teaching young people about the genocide and promoting a culture of peace. Schools incorporate lessons on the dangers of hate speech, the importance of unity, and the value of reconciliation. Such education initiatives are essential for breaking the cycle of violence and creating a generation committed to tolerance and human dignity.

Alison Des Forges underscores the importance of education, writing, "Teaching about genocide is not only about remembering the past but also about shaping a future that rejects hatred and embraces diversity" (Des Forges, 1999, p. 517). The inclusion of genocide education in national curricula worldwide can help raise awareness about the consequences of discrimination, intolerance, and dehumanization, fostering a global culture that values human rights.

Rwanda's approach to education can serve as a model for other countries. Philip Gourevitch notes, "By confronting the past openly, Rwanda is instilling in its young people the knowledge and responsibility to prevent history from repeating itself" (Gourevitch, 1998, p. 326). Expanding genocide education globally and integrating it into educational systems can help create a more informed and compassionate world.

Supporting Civil Society and Grassroots Movements

Civil society organizations and grassroots movements play a critical role in advocating for human rights, monitoring potential abuses, and mobilizing public support for intervention. These organizations often operate in situations where governments may be unwilling or unable to act, providing an essential voice for marginalized communities. Supporting civil society is crucial for building resilience within societies and enabling early responses to signs of potential genocide.

Samantha Power highlights the impact of civil society, writing, "Civil society organizations can be the first line of defense against mass atrocities, raising alarms and advocating for those who are most vulnerable" (Power, 2002, p. 525). Encouraging the growth of civil society, particularly in fragile states, can help build local capacity to identify and address human rights abuses before they escalate into violence.

However, civil society organizations often face challenges, including limited funding, government restrictions, and threats to activists. Mahmood Mamdani emphasizes, "Supporting civil society requires not only financial resources but also a commitment to protecting the space in which these organizations operate" (Mamdani, 2001, p. 438). By empowering civil society, the international community can strengthen grassroots efforts to prevent genocide.

The Role of Global Solidarity and Moral Responsibility

Ultimately, preventing genocide requires a commitment to global solidarity and a recognition of our shared moral responsibility. The failure to prevent the Rwandan genocide demonstrated the consequences of moral indifference and the dangers of prioritizing national interests over human lives. Building a world where genocide is unthinkable demands a collective commitment to protecting the most vulnerable, regardless of borders or political considerations.

Roméo Dallaire reflects on this moral imperative, stating, "The world's failure in Rwanda was not just a political failure; it was a moral failure. To prevent future genocides, we must find the courage to stand up for humanity, even when it is inconvenient or difficult" (Dallaire, 2003, p. 392). The principle of "Never Again" requires more than words—it requires action, empathy, and a willingness to intervene in the face of atrocity.

Global solidarity also means supporting countries in post-conflict recovery, providing assistance for rebuilding, reconciliation, and justice. Linda Melvern writes, "Preventing genocide is not only about stopping violence but also about supporting societies in healing and rebuilding after atrocity" (Melvern, 2000, p. 540). The international community has a role to play in helping nations recover and ensuring that the conditions for genocide are never allowed to re-emerge.

Conclusion: Building a Future Free from Genocide

The lessons of the Rwandan genocide compel the world to act with urgency and commitment to prevent future atrocities. The principles of early intervention, international justice, education, and global solidarity provide a foundation for building a world where genocide is truly unthinkable. However, these principles must be backed by political will, resources, and a shared recognition of our moral responsibility.

Samantha Power captures this challenge, writing, "The promise of 'Never Again' must be more than a slogan. It must be a call to action that drives us to build institutions, strengthen alliances, and stand together in defense of human rights" (Power, 2002, p. 547). The legacy of Rwanda is a reminder that the cost of inaction is far too high, and that the international community must rise to the challenge of preventing future genocides.

As the world reflects on Rwanda's experience, it is clear that preventing genocide is a shared duty that requires vigilance, empathy, and resolve. Roméo Dallaire's words resonate as a call to action: "We must be prepared to stand against hate, to protect the innocent, and to act when others turn away. This is the legacy of Rwanda, and it is our responsibility to honor it" (Dallaire, 2003, p. 414). The path forward is challenging, but by embracing these lessons, the world can work toward a future where genocide truly becomes a relic of the past.

References

- Dallaire, Roméo. *Shake Hands with the Devil: The Failure of Humanity in Rwanda*. Random House Canada, 2003.
- Des Forges, Alison. *Leave None to Tell the Story: Genocide in Rwanda*. Human Rights Watch, 1999.
- Gourevitch, Philip. *We Wish to Inform You That Tomorrow We Will Be Killed with Our Families: Stories from Rwanda*. Picador, 1998.
- Mamdani, Mahmood. *When Victims Become Killers: Colonialism, Nativism, and the Genocide in Rwanda*. Princeton University Press, 2001.
- Melvern, Linda. *A People Betrayed: The Role of the West in Rwanda's Genocide*. Zed Books, 2000.
- Power, Samantha. *A Problem from Hell: America and the Age of Genocide*. Basic Books, 2002.
- Straus, Scott. *The Order of Genocide: Race, Power, and War in Rwanda*. Cornell University Press, 2006.

13

Conclusion

The Price of Silence and the Call for Change

The Rwandan genocide stands as one of the most haunting examples of what can happen when the international community fails to act in the face of mass atrocity. The tragedy unfolded over 100 days in 1994, claiming the lives of nearly one million people, while the world largely watched in silence. The horrors that took place in Rwanda continue to resonate, serving as a somber reminder of the consequences of global inaction. This conclusion reflects on the price of that silence, the imperative to renew our commitment to human rights, and the vision for a world where the promise of "Never Again" is upheld.

Summarizing the Consequences of Global Inaction

The inaction of the international community during the Rwandan genocide is a lesson in the devastating cost of apathy, bureaucratic delays, and political caution. Despite clear warnings from within Rwanda and numerous reports from human rights organizations, the world's major powers failed to intervene. The reasons for this inaction were complex: the scars of previous peacekeeping failures, the prioritization of national interests over humanitarian needs, and the entrenched principle of state sovereignty, which became a convenient shield behind which nations could hide their reluctance.

Roméo Dallaire, who led the United Nations Assistance Mission for Rwanda (UNAMIR), spoke extensively about the frustration he felt in his pleas for help being ignored. In his words, "We had the knowledge and the capacity to prevent a genocide, yet the political will was absent. The price of that silence is a scar on humanity that can never fully heal" (Dallaire, 2003, p. 404). Dallaire's sentiments highlight the fact that while military and logistical support may have been limited, it was ultimately the lack of moral courage that allowed the genocide to unfold unimpeded.

The consequences of this inaction went beyond the immediate loss of life. The genocide destabilized the entire Great Lakes region, leading to waves of refugees, regional conflicts, and an enduring legacy of trauma for survivors. Samantha Power reflects on the ripple effects of the genocide, noting, "The failure to act in Rwanda sent a message to perpetrators worldwide that the world would turn a blind eye to mass violence, as long as it was contained within national borders" (Power, 2002, p. 553). This inaction created an environment where mass murder could occur with impunity, underscoring the urgent need for a more robust and morally centered approach to international relations.

Furthermore, the Rwandan genocide exposed the weaknesses within international institutions like the United Nations, which was hamstrung by political divisions, limited resources, and restrictive mandates. The UN's failure to protect Rwandans shattered the credibility of global institutions tasked with maintaining peace and security, leading to a wave of reform initiatives aimed at preventing future genocides. Philip Gourevitch captures this institutional failing: "In Rwanda, the world's promises to uphold human rights and protect innocent lives were revealed as hollow. The institutional silence was as deafening as the cries for help that went unanswered" (Gourevitch, 1998, p. 344).

Renewing the Commitment to Human Rights

The Rwandan genocide has compelled the international community to reassess its approach to human rights and humanitarian intervention. In the aftermath, a renewed commitment to human rights was seen in the development of frameworks like the Responsibility to Protect (R2P), which seeks to redefine state sovereignty as a responsibility to protect citizens, rather than a shield for impunity. R2P emerged from the understanding that sovereignty cannot be used as an excuse for inaction in the face of mass atrocities. As Mahmood Mamdani argues, "Rwanda forced the world to recognize that sovereignty, while crucial, cannot come at the expense of human life" (Mamdani, 2001, p. 468).

However, renewing the commitment to human rights goes beyond creating doctrines; it requires political will, resources, and a shift in how the world prioritizes humanitarian concerns over national interests. To honor this commitment, governments must be willing to act swiftly and decisively, recognizing that a delay in intervention can be the difference between life and death. Samantha Power points out that "True commitment to human rights means being willing to make difficult choices and to place human dignity above geopolitical calculations" (Power, 2002, p. 567).

Renewing this commitment also entails supporting international institutions like the International Criminal Court (ICC), which aims to hold perpetrators of genocide, war crimes, and crimes against humanity accountable. Accountability is a critical component of preventing future atrocities, as it reinforces the notion that those who commit mass atrocities will face justice. The establishment of the ICC and the strengthening of human rights institutions are steps toward ensuring that the world can respond more effectively to threats of genocide. Linda Melvern argues, "Justice must be a pillar of any human rights agenda. Without accountability, the promise of 'Never Again' is little more than a hollow declaration" (Melvern, 2000, p. 582).

Moreover, renewing the commitment to human rights includes educating the public and promoting awareness about the warning signs of genocide and the importance of intervention. The collective memory of the Rwandan genocide must be preserved, not only to honor the victims but also to ensure that future generations understand the consequences of silence and indifference. In Rwanda, memorials, museums, and educational programs keep the memory of the genocide alive, serving as both a warning and a call to action. Alison Des Forges emphasizes, "The memory of Rwanda's tragedy is a moral compass for humanity, reminding us that complacency and ignorance can be as deadly as the perpetrators themselves" (Des Forges, 1999, p. 532).

A Vision for a World Where "Never Again" Holds True

The phrase "Never Again" became a rallying cry after the Holocaust, yet Rwanda demonstrated that the international community had not fully internalized this promise. If the world is to ensure that "Never Again" holds true, it must be prepared to act with urgency and conviction in the face of potential genocide. This vision requires a reimagining of international relations, where human rights are not secondary to state sovereignty, and where intervention in the face of atrocity is seen as a moral imperative, not a political option.

A world where "Never Again" holds true would be one in which early warning systems are not merely symbolic but are equipped with the resources and authority to respond to crises. It would mean that countries are willing to support rapid-response peacekeeping forces that can be deployed at the first signs of mass violence. Roméo Dallaire argues for this kind of proactive approach, stating, "The greatest lesson from Rwanda is that prevention requires both readiness and resolve. The world cannot wait until the killing begins to mobilize; it must be prepared to act at the first signs of danger" (Dallaire, 2003, p. 419).

This vision also calls for a stronger and more unified international community that prioritizes human rights. Organizations like the United Nations, regional bodies, and human rights NGOs must work in concert, sharing information and resources to prevent crises before they escalate. Philip Gourevitch envisions this ideal, noting, "A world truly committed to 'Never Again' would be one where institutions of power serve as guardians of peace and protectors of the vulnerable, bound not by politics but by a shared humanity" (Gourevitch, 1998, p. 362).

Finally, achieving a world where "Never Again" holds true requires a cultural shift—one that promotes empathy, awareness, and a deep-seated respect for human life across borders. Education must play a central role in fostering this shift. Teaching about past genocides, promoting intercultural understanding, and addressing the root causes of hatred and division can help build societies that are resilient against the forces of extremism and intolerance. Linda Melvern emphasizes this point, stating, "Building a world free from genocide means building a world that values compassion, inclusivity, and the dignity of every individual" (Melvern, 2000, p. 601).

The commitment to "Never Again" is not a destination but an ongoing journey. It requires vigilance, a willingness to learn from the past, and the courage to confront the forces of hatred whenever they arise. Rwanda's legacy calls the world to action, demanding that the international community take responsibility for the well-being of all humanity. Samantha Power concludes, "The promise of 'Never Again' will only hold true if we, as a global community, recognize our interconnectedness and accept the responsibility to protect one another, even when it is difficult or inconvenient" (Power, 2002, p. 574).

Final Reflection: Answering the Call

The Rwandan genocide stands as a stark reminder of the price of silence and the moral cost of indifference. It serves as a call for change—a call to build a world where human rights are upheld, where the vulnerable are protected, and where the memory of those who suffered serves as a guide for future action. Rwanda's journey from tragedy to resilience offers hope, but it also places a responsibility on the shoulders of the international community.

If "Never Again" is to be more than a mere slogan, it must be an active commitment—a promise to act, to protect, and to preserve the sanctity of human life. Rwanda's past calls on us to confront injustice wherever it arises, to speak out against hatred, and to hold ourselves accountable to the values of compassion and courage. The world has been given a chance to learn from Rwanda, and it is up to each of us to answer that call with resolve, empathy, and unwavering dedication to the cause of humanity.

In the words of Roméo Dallaire, "If we are to honor those who perished in Rwanda, we must strive to build a world where silence is never the answer and where justice, peace, and human dignity prevail" (Dallaire, 2003, p. 430). This is the legacy of Rwanda—a reminder that in the face of darkness, the light of compassion and action must shine brighter than ever.

Don't miss out!

Visit the website below and you can sign up to receive emails whenever Kayumba David publishes a new book. There's no charge and no obligation.

https://books2read.com/r/B-A-KRSOC-RYRFF

BOOKS 2 READ

Connecting independent readers to independent writers.

Did you love *Silent Complicity: State Sovereignty, Global Inaction, and the Rwandan Genocide*? Then you should read *Grow a Backbone and Walk Out: The Guide to Escaping Your Abusive Marriage* by Kayumba David and Rachael Nyarangi!

Grow a Backbone and Walk out of an Abusive Marriage

Rachael Nyarangi & Kay

This book is not just about leaving an abusive marriage; it is about reclaiming your life and finding your true self. It is about understanding that no cultural or religious doctrine should ever condone your suffering. It is about recognizing that you deserve love, respect, and happiness. Through practical advice, emotional support, and a touch of humor, this guide aims to empower you to take the necessary steps towards freedom.